Jericho

*Dead
Sea*

...f Olives

● Bethany

▲
●
Jerusalem

●
Bethlehem

●
Emmaus

IDUMEA

JUDEA

—

WHERE JESUS WALKED

BY ROY SCHWARCZ
AND JONATHAN SINGER

"I AM NOT A BELIEVER. BUT I MUST CONFESS
AS AN HISTORIAN, THIS PENNILESS CREATURE FROM
GALILEE IS IRRESISTIBLY THE CENTER OF HISTORY."

H.G. Wells
Historian & Author

EXECUTIVE EDITOR
Albert J. Nader

EDITORS
James Vincent
Becky Kavka

PRODUCTION DIRECTOR
Phillip Pecelunas

PRODUCTION MANAGER
Melody Hazen

ORIGINAL PHOTOGRAPHY
Israel Talby

ADDITIONAL PHOTOGRAPHY
ASAP Jerusalem
Garo Nalbandian, Richard Nowitz,
Sammy Avnisan, Aliza Auerbach,
Mike Ganor, Lex Borodulin,
Avi Hirschfield, Eitan Simanor

PICTURE EDITORS
Melody Hazen
Jeff Tarkington

DESIGN
William Hollingshead
Del Larkin

Published by Epoch Books,
a division of Questar, Inc.
680 N. Lake Shore Drive,
Chicago, IL 60611
(312) 266-9400

Printed and bound in the USA by
Rand McNally & Company

Library of Congress Catalog
Card Number: 95-61933

ISBN 1-56855-114-2

CONTENTS

PREFACE

This is a book worthy of your attention.

The Swedish film director, Igmar Bergman, dreamed that he was standing in a cathedral in Europe looking at a painting of Christ. Desperate to hear a word from outside his own world, he visualized himself shouting, "Speak to me!"

Dead silence.

That, we are told, was the inspiration for his movie *Silence,* which portrayed people who despaired of finding God. In our world, he believed, we only hear ourselves. No voice comes from outside the human predicament. When seeking a word from God, we are confronted with dead calm.

This book, *Where Jesus Walked,* confidently affirms that God has spoken. Through the prophets and teachers of the Old Testament, and later through Christ who fulfilled the Messianic predictions, God has spoken and He has not stuttered.

As you read these pages, keep in mind that Christ, unlike other teachers, constantly pressed the question of what people thought of Him. "Who do *men* say that I am?" was quickly followed by a personal question to His disciples, "Who do *you* say that I am?"

Christ pressed the question for one good reason: He taught that what men thought of Him determined their eternal destiny!

Where Jesus Walked presents a portrait of Christ that grows out of the Old Testament prophecies and is confirmed by His words and His works. You will be surprised at how many ancient predictions were specifically fulfilled with an accuracy that cannot be explained by coincidence.

Regardless of your personal opinion about Christ, you will have to agree that His claims stand unrivaled. In fact, the more we know Him, the more convinced we become that He cannot be placed on the same level with other prophets or gurus, no matter how great. Read this book and you will better understand why the Christ of the New Testament has no serious rivals.

Let's take a moment to reflect on what Christ claimed.

During the Russian Revolution of 1918, Lenin said that if Communism were in power, there would be bread for every household, yet he never had the nerve to say, *"I am the bread of life; he who comes to Me shall not hunger, and he who believes in Me shall never thirst"* (John 6:35).

Hitler made astounding claims for the role of Germany and the Reich of the future, yet he never said of himself, *"I am the way the truth and the life; no man cometh unto the Father but by me"* (John 14:6).

Freud believed that psychotherapy would heal people's emotional and spiritual pains. But he could not say, *"Peace I leave with you; not as the world gives, do I give you. Let not your heart be troubled, nor let it be fearful"* (John 11:25).

Mystics claim enlightenment, yet I have never read of one who said, *"I am the light of the world; he who follows Me shall not walk in darkness, but shall have the light of life"* (John 8:12).

New Age gurus say that some day we will all be reincarnated, yet none of them can say, *"I am the resurrection and the life; he that believeth in Me though he were dead, yet shall he live; and whosoever liveth and believeth in Me shall never die"* (John 11:25).

As a delegate to the Parliament to World Religions, which met in Chicago in 1993, I walked through the display area where the religions of the world were represented. I went from booth to booth asking the different delegates if their particular religion had a Savior who claimed to have the ability to forgive sins and lead us to God. Not one met my challenge. Each religion had prophets and gurus aplenty, but these enlightened teachers, I discovered, were flawed just like us. Since they shared in our predicament as sinners, they could neither save themselves or us.

Many years ago, a celebrated painting by Burne-Jones named *Love Among Ruins* was destroyed by an art firm that had been hired to restore it. Though they were warned that it was a watercolor and needed special attention, they used the wrong formula and dissolved the paint.

Throughout the ages, men have taken the New Testament portrait of Christ and have tried to reduce its bright hues to gray tints; they have attempted to make Christ into a mere man and reinterpret his claims. So far, however, no one has found the solvent needed to neutralize the original and reduce it to dull canvas. No matter who has tried to blend its hues to match that of ordinary men, the portrait remains stubborn, immune to those who wish to transform it to their own liking.

Poor Igmar Bergman! We sympathize with his desire to hear God; but rather than listen for His whisper in an empty cathedral, he should have heard His megaphone on the pages of the Old and New Testaments! No wonder Christ was fond of chiding His listeners by saying, *"He that has ears, let him hear!"*

Kingdoms come and go, but Christ lives. Centuries come and go, but Christ lives. Kings are crowned and uncrowned, but Christ lives. Emperors decree His extinction, but yet Christ lives. He is the one enduring figure of history; the One whose claim to eternal existence has the ring of integrity.

You are about to embark on a journey that will begin with the birth of Christ and end with His ascension into heaven. You will see where He walked and lived. If you are a cynic, your skepticism will be challenged. If you already are a believer in Christ, your faith will be strengthened.

Keep reading.

Dr. Erwin W. Lutzer
Senior Pastor, The Moody Church
Chicago, Illinois

INTRODUCTION

The land of Israel holds an irresistible attraction to the people of the world. The city of Jerusalem, nestled in the heart of a picturesque mosaic of deep ravines and rugged hills, is sacred to three of the world's great religions: Christianity, Judaism, and Islam. "The future of Jerusalem," said one observer, with slight exaggeration, "is the future of the world."

The past and the present come together in Israel as perhaps nowhere else in the world. Jesus walked where Abraham, Joshua and Samson had lived centuries earlier. Here Christ meets King David; the Apostle Peter stood where the prophet Isaiah had his visions of Israel's glorious future many generations before.

Today the land of ancient prophets is home to modern zealots who believe that the coming of a Messiah might just be around the corner. While the ruins of ancient temples are excavated, a few present-day visionaries are making plans to build a new temple in anticipation of a glorious new age. All of this in a land that has known more wars than historians care to recount.

What you hold in your hands is our attempt to illustrate by pictures and commentary the unique relationship Christ has with both the Old and New Testaments. He is the bridge that spans the centuries, erasing the neat division that is often made between the two parts of what we call The Bible. We are convinced that the sage was right when he said: "The New is in the Old concealed and the Old is in the New revealed!"

Many books have been written about where Jesus walked. But we believe ours is different because we have included a sampling of Jewish, Christian and secular references. We have painstakingly researched the events in the life of Christ with the help of Israeli photographers who have verified the various sites as reliably as possible. Most importantly, we have tried to allow Jewish customs and traditions shed light on the life of Christ. This is not merely a book that shows us where Jesus walked. It is a book that attempts to let us understand who Jesus is.

Jesus himself challenged His critics to "search the Scriptures," for in doing so, they would discover that "they testify of Me." Moses, the prophets, David — all of these men predicted a coming Messiah. Taking up His challenge, we have connected each of the major events of His life with an Old and New Testament "link."

How best to use this book?

We suggest that you resist the temptation to hurriedly scan these pages. Take time to absorb the pictures and give some thought to the ties between the Old and the New.

Of course it would be a much deeper and insightful experience to actually visit Israel than to simply see photographs of the land. But the wise arm-chair traveler will be able to capture some of the meaning and importance of these special places by careful reading and observation.

Since most of the Bible is in narrative, these real-life stories touch us at the deepest level of human need and emotion. Whether it is Abraham's willingness to sacrifice his son, Isaac, or Christ's terrified disciples trying to sail to safety on the Galilee, the Bible, unlike most other books, invites us to personally relive these events as we remember that God is with us, just as He was with His people so many centuries ago.

This book was birthed in the mind of Albert Nader, an Elder at the Moody Church in Chicago. For years he had been impressed with the relationship between the predictions about the Messiah in the Old Testament and their fulfillment in Christ. He saw that the gulf which often, and unfortunately, exists between Judaism and Christianity could be bridged only if the Old and New Testaments were not viewed as two separate books, but as a single, unified message. He challenged us to search intensively to find the parallels which exist between the two halves of the Bible. I might add that Mr. Nader often reminded us that his ancestors, like Abraham, were originally Chaldeans from the Assyria!

Perhaps it is not even necessary to mention our hopes that you read this book with an open mind. Whatever your religious beliefs or background, we think you will agree that Christ transcends all cultures and continents with a message for the peoples of this world.

Regardless of what you think of Christ, we hope this book will challenge you to have a more informed opinion about Him. We think you will concur that He cannot easily be ignored or reinterpreted to fit our preconceived notions of who He might be.

Come with us on a journey that combines history, religion and biography into one unified story which begins at the Garden of Eden and ends just beyond the Garden of Gethsemane. Bring your faith and your doubts.

Let us walk together.

Roy Schwarcz
Jonathan Singer

A SURPRISE ANNOUNCEMENT
MATTHEW 1:18-25

Old Testament Link

The virgin birth of a Messiah was prophesied more than 700 years before the actual birth of Jesus. Through Isaiah, God gave the king of Judah assurance that his enemies would not prevail against him. Simultaneously, Isaiah foretold the coming of the Messiah through a miraculous birth (Isaiah 7:14-16). The great prophesy of the Messiah came in the first verse: "Therefore the Lord himself will give you a sign: The virgin will be with child and will give birth to a son, and will call him Immanuel."

When Joseph of Nazareth discovered that Mary (Miriam in Hebrew), his betrothed, was pregnant, he was heartbroken. He could only conclude that she had been unfaithful to him, perhaps during her visit to Judea with her relative, Elizabeth, the mother of John the Baptist.

In the days of Jesus, betrothal was equated with marriage, so any unfaithfulness was shocking, even devastating. As was the custom, Joseph's father had probably selected a wife for his son, and had an agreement drawn up to cover the details, including the amount of the dowry. The contract was then sealed. In the bride's house the betrothal ceremony was enacted under a small canopy; this ceremony was called the "making sacred." From this point onward, Mary, as the betrothed woman, was considered sacred to her husband-to-be. Only death or divorce could sever the two.

Imagine Joseph's shock to learn his betrothed was pregnant. He had only two options. Punishment for her infidelity would have been death by stoning, as decreed by Mosaic Law. The other option was to divorce her quietly. Joseph seriously considered this option, for he did not want to expose her to public disgrace.

No human counsel could illuminate Joseph's mind nor soothe his heart. As Joseph anguished over his decision, an angel of the Lord appeared to him in a dream. "Joseph, son of David, do not be afraid to take Mary home as your wife, because what is conceived in her is from the Holy Spirit."

The dream gave him a sense of calm. He would marry his betrothed, but would have "no union with her until she gave birth to a son."

New Testament Fulfillment

Jesus had to be born of a virgin to fulfill the prophecy of Isaiah (Matthew 1:22-23). But a virgin birth also was necessary to allow God to become a man, born of flesh, yet without the stain of sin. This miraculous birth was a sign to Israel that God was now dwelling among them.

Today Old Nazareth is gone, but a Galilean road similar to this led to the town that gave the world Jesus.

JOURNEY TO BETHLEHEM
LUKE 2:1-5

Old Testament Link

The town was "small among Judah," but Bethlehem was where the Messiah would be born, according to the prophet Micah: "But you, Bethlehem Ephrathah, though you are small among the clans of Judah, out of you will come for me one who will be ruler over Israel, whose origins are from of old, from ancient times" (Micah 5:2). Rabbinic sources agree this was a prediction of the Messiah's birthplace. But why would Mary and Joseph, living in Galilee, return to the home of their forefather, David?

A sage once said that a coincidence is a miracle of God in which He chooses to remain anonymous. The prophet Micah stated the Messiah was to be born in Bethlehem. Yet Joseph and his betrothed lived in Galilee. Only the decree of Caesar Augustus for all citizens to return to their ancestral homeland to be counted in a census could induce Joseph to take his pregnant wife on such a hazardous journey. But the unforeseen hand of God was moving so "that all might be fulfilled."

Bethlehem was the ancestral home of both Mary and Joseph; both were descendants of King David. Aside from the hazardous journey, the prospect of settling permanently in Bethlehem, the land of their fathers, may have appealed to both Joseph and Mary.

Today, the journey from Nazareth to Bethlehem takes about two hours by car. Two thousand years ago, the 90-mile trip could have taken as long as two weeks. The coolness of the season probably made the trip even more difficult.

As the weary couple approached the city of their ancestors, their spirits rallied with thoughts connected with their hometown: Rachel, Ruth, Naomi, Boaz and Jesse were all buried there.

Joseph and Mary probably went first to a Jewish home to stay, as was the local custom for those in need. But because the city was already filled with visitors, an innkeeper may have offered them the only space he had left; a courtyard enclosure where animals were kept. Here they would have their firstborn son.

The countryside surrounding Bethlehem looks much like it did when Joseph and Mary arrived from Nazareth. Bethlehem is a small town five miles south of Jerusalem. It sits on a ridge over 2000 feet above sea level.

New Testament Fulfillment
The Roman Emperor Caesar Augustus decreed a worldwide census, and every man had to return to his birthplace to register. Thus Joseph had to expose Mary to a perilous journey to Bethlehem. There, in the little town that in Hebrew means "house of bread," Jesus was born, who would be known as the Bread of Life (John 6:35).

THE SHEPHERDS
LUKE 2:8-20

Old Testament Link

The shepherds of the Christmas story were not the first men of their humble occupation to be chosen by God. King David also began his life of glory and greatness as a shepherd. And to King David, God promised an offspring who would be the promised Messiah and Deliverer (2 Samuel 7:12-15). When the prophet Samuel was sent by God to anoint a new man to be king in Israel, David's father didn't even consider his youngest, who was thought to be the least important in the family. Yet this son, a shepherd boy, would become Israel's greatest king. Centuries later, God chose the ordinary shepherds to be the first witnesses of the birth of Israel's ultimate King.

God drew wise men from the east to herald the coming of His Son, but He also announced this extraordinary event to shepherds tending their flocks in the fields.

Why were these shepherds chosen? Perhaps these young men were Levitical shepherds charged with guarding the sheep for the sacrifices in nearby Jerusalem. Such shepherds were descendants of Temple Priests and made sure the sheep they protected would not eat anything that would make them impure.

Yet, ironically, these shepherds were considered socially inferior. Shepherds were not even allowed to enter the Temple courts.

What a picture of God's grace; lowly shepherds were the first invited to behold God's Messiah. God had revealed Himself to the ordinary; He lifted up the humble while ignoring the proud.

If these shepherds were the Levites who guarded the sacrificial lambs, they were the first chosen to behold another sacrificial lamb; Jesus. Isaiah the prophet described the Messiah as a lamb who, when being sheared of wool, would not open its mouth. Upon seeing Jesus for the first time, John the Baptist would later cry: "Look, the Lamb of God!" (John 1:36).

The appearance of an angel and "the glory of the Lord" terrified the shepherds. "The glory of the Lord" is a reference to the Shechinah, a cloud of intolerable brightness; the same glory that filled the Temple on the day that Solomon dedicated it (2 Chronicles 7). Then, after 1500 years, the glory of the Lord appeared proclaiming the promised Messiah. Years later the same heavenly glory would overwhelm the disciples on the Mount of Transfiguration.

Even today, the hills around Bethlehem are dotted with sheep, goats and shepherds.

New Testament Fulfillment

After the angels heralded "good news of great joy" that a "Savior has been born to you," the shepherds hurried to discover the baby lying in a manger, with his parents looking on (Luke 2:8-11, 16). The Scripture says that the shepherds returned "glorifying and praising God" (Luke 2:20). Though just an infant, the Messiah could inspire joy, even in the hearts of lowly shepherds.

11

NO ROOM AT THE INN
LUKE 2:6-7

Old Testament Link

The prophet Isaiah had foretold that the coming Messiah would be "...oppressed and afflicted, yet he did not open his mouth; he was led like a lamb to the slaughter, and as a sheep before her shearers is silent, so he did not open his mouth" (Isaiah 53:7). Jesus was God's perfect sacrificial Lamb. Born in a place where animals were kept, cradled in a feeding trough, He was viewed by lowly shepherds. All the signs of the Messiah predicted by the Old Testament prophets pointed to Jesus as the Lamb of God.

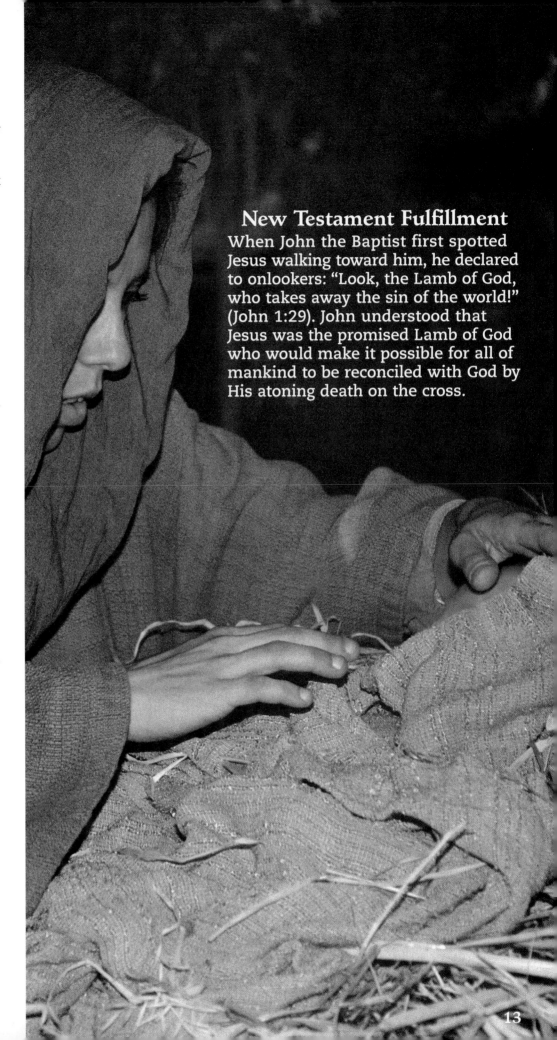

Everything about Jesus' birth — His earthly parents, the time, the place — occurred with divine precision. The time was perfectly synchronized with the timetable in Daniel (Daniel 9:24). His parents were descendants of King David, a prerequisite. And Jesus was born in Bethlehem, fulfilling Micah's prophecy about the Messiah's birthplace.

Neither kingly garments nor hand servants would attend His birth. The stable may have even been a cave that sheltered animals, as some historians believe.

These shelters with large recesses often housed travelers and provided an enclosure for their animals. On these crude floors, travelers would spread their rugs, for these cave-like dwellings offered few basic comforts. Joseph and Mary, finding even these lodgings occupied, were forced to look for shelter among the animals.

This was where the Messiah was born. Wrapped in ordinary strips of cloth, the baby Jesus might have resembled a mummy wrapped for burial. This image of the Child born-to-die would reappear for those that remembered seeing Him then, His first hour of life.

His first public presentation was his circumcision eight days later in the Temple at Jerusalem. Sixty days later, according to the Law, every firstborn male was to be redeemed from the Lord's priestly service. Not only did the mother of Jesus need to bring a sacrifice for her own ceremonial defilement of childbirth (a reference to mankind's birth in sin), she and Joseph were also required to furnish an offering for the Redemption of the First Born.

Some 30 years later, Jesus returned to the Temple to make the ultimate offering of Himself for the redemption of every person who would believe in Him.

Located near Bethlehem, Jesus was probably born in a cave where animals were often sheltered.

New Testament Fulfillment

When John the Baptist first spotted Jesus walking toward him, he declared to onlookers: "Look, the Lamb of God, who takes away the sin of the world!" (John 1:29). John understood that Jesus was the promised Lamb of God who would make it possible for all of mankind to be reconciled with God by His atoning death on the cross.

THE VISIT BY WISE MEN
MATTHEW 2:1-2, 7-12

Old Testament Link

Hundreds of years before the Messiah's birth in Bethlehem, God placed clues for the wise men to follow. The prophets Balaam and Daniel, both living in the east, left a clear record of prophecy concerning the times and circumstances surrounding the Messiah's coming (Numbers 24:17; Daniel 9:25). All the wise men had to do was be obedient and follow.

Tradition tells us there were *three* wise men, but the Bible is not specific, nor does any passage in the Scripture reveal these men were kings. We do know that they were from the east. When Scripture mentions the east it is usually referring to Assyria or Babylon, today known as Iran and Iraq. In the Assyrian town of Saba near Teheran, Marco Polo was once shown three well-preserved bodies. Still with hair and beards, they were grandly entombed. These men were said to be Balthasar, Gaspar and Melchior, the wise men from the town of Saba. It was from Saba it is believed that they traveled to Bethlehem.

What exactly were wise men? The word *Magi* is a Greek term for wise men, or more specifically, astrologers. These men studied the heavens for clues to man's worldly fortunes. But even this does not explain how these Babylonian astrologers became interested in a Jewish Messiah. There are two possible explanations.

First, they could have been familiar with the writings of Daniel and his prophecies concerning the timing of the Messiah's coming.

Second, they might have known about Balaam's prophecy of a star coming from Judah, another reference to the Messiah. Balaam was from Pethor, a city on the banks of the Euphrates River in Babylon (Numbers 22:5; Deuteronomy 23:4). It is a possibility that these wise men also knew of Balaam's writings.

"...the star they had seen in the east went ahead of them until it stopped over the place the young child was." Since the star led them it was likely no ordinary light. The Greek word for star is radiance or brilliance. Appearing, disappearing and leading them, this was no star. In all likelihood, this was the very Shechinah glory of God's presence guiding them! (Exodus 19:18, 40:38).

The roads that lead to Bethlehem are much like they were 2000 years ago when Magi came to worship Jesus.

New Testament Fulfillment

The Magi were the first in a long line of kings and princes who would come to worship the baby that was born in the manger of Bethlehem. The wise men recognized him as a king. The apostles Paul and John both described the risen Jesus as King of kings and Lord of lords (1 Timothy 6:14-15; Revelation 17:14).

15

FLIGHT INTO EGYPT
MATTHEW 2:13-21

Old Testament Link

Hosea foretold Jesus' leaving Egypt, writing "When Israel was a child, I loved him, and out of Egypt I called my son" (Hosea 11:1). God had a special place in His heart for Egypt because of the country's early blessing to the sons of Jacob and for being the sanctuary for the Messiah. In the coming Messianic Kingdom, Egypt will be blessed by the Lord (Isaiah 19:23-25).

Desperate for recognition and glory, King Herod the Great, the mixed-blood despot, assured himself a place in history. He did this not by virtue of his genius, military know-how, or benevolence. Sadly, King Herod is mostly remembered for one of the most heinous acts in all of history, the Slaughter of the Innocents.

Herod, the Roman-appointed King of the Jews, feared any threat to his throne. He killed one of his wives and children thinking they were plotting against him. Suspecting that the wise men had ignored his wishes to lead him to the infant Messiah, Herod ordered the execution of all male children under the age of two in Bethlehem.

Joseph had been warned in a dream by an angel of the Lord and had taken Mary and the Child to Egypt. Through this act, Matthew saw the fulfillment of the Old Testament prophecy: "...out of Egypt I called my Son." He also saw the fulfillment of Jeremiah's prophecy of Rachel weeping for her children (Jeremiah 31:15).

In quoting the weeping prophet Jeremiah, Matthew foresaw not only the tragedy in Bethlehem, but also the continuing tribulation of Israel.

Based on Bethlehem's relatively small population, historians estimate the number of infants killed at no more than 20. Yet the number of these innocent children does not reduce the terrible cruelty of the crime, nor downplay their commemoration for all eternity.

After Herod's death, an angel again spoke to Joseph. It was safe to leave Egypt. Joseph and Mary could return to Israel to resume a normal life — raising the future Messiah in Nazareth!

Traveling to Egypt was not unusual for Joseph and Mary. There were several Jewish colonies in major cities at that time.

New Testament Fulfillment

Matthew saw the fulfillment of Hosea's prophecy concerning Israel and the promised Messiah: "...where he stayed until the death of Herod. And so was fulfilled what the Lord had said through the prophet: 'Out of Egypt I called my son'" (Matthew 2:15). Although the context of Hosea's prophecy refers to the state of Israel when God brought the Jews out of bondage, the Holy Spirit through Matthew applied this also to Jesus and His return to the land of Israel after the death of Herod.

RETURN TO GALILEE
MATTHEW 2:22-23

Old Testament Link

Jesus grew up in the town of Nazareth, located in Galilee, a land that the prophets assigned no special place in history. Yet, in Isaiah 9:1-2, a startling prediction was made for the region of Galilee: "a great light" would appear. Those who were religious thought little of anyone who came from the Land of the Gentiles. Isaiah also foretold that the promised Messiah would be despised and forsaken by men (Isaiah 53:3).

Far from the greeting card vision of the holy family peacefully treading moonlit hills westward, their flight to Egypt was probably undertaken with great haste and fear.

His body wracked with disease and knowing his death was near, Herod the Great lashed out with his final misdeed: the Slaughter of the Innocents. He followed this act by burning alive two of Israel's most beloved rabbis and 40 of their followers. He also ordered the exe-cution of his own son, Herod Antipas.

When Herod's evil tyrany had finally ended and he had died, an angel told Joseph to leave Egypt and return to Israel, but not back to Bethlehem, the town of his ancestors. Instead, he was directed to Nazareth, away from Herod's son and cruel successor, Archelaus. This was to fulfill what the prophets had foretold, that the Messiah would be a Nazarene.

Nazareth, located in the heart of Galilee, was despised by the Jewish community as a Gentile stronghold. Compared to the religious piety of Jerusalem's residents, the Galileans were irreligious and held in disdain by much of the nation.

Jesus' identification with Galilee and the lonely fishermen who worked the Sea of Galilee was further cause for the Jewish people to dislike Him. Thus He grew up in what was then known as the "Land

New Testament Fulfillment

Jesus the Galilean was despised by the "religious" men of His day, especially because He grew up in Nazareth located in Galilee. We see this in the response of Nathanael when told by Philip that Jesus of Nazareth was the Messiah and Nathaniel's reply was: "Can anything good come from there?" Philip said to him: "Come and see." Indeed a new spiritual light was shining (John 1:46).

of the Gentiles," fulfilling Isaiah's prophecy: "In the past he humbled the land of Zebulun and the land of Naphtali, but in the future he will honor Galilee of the Gentiles, by the way of the sea, along the Jordan — the people walking in darkness have seen a great light; on those living in the land of the shadow of death a light has dawned" (Isaiah 9:1-2).

The source of this "great light" would be the birth of the "Wonderful Counselor, Mighty God, Everlasting Father, Prince of Peace," who would "reign on David's throne" (Isaiah 9:6-7).

Joseph and Mary were warned in a dream to leave Egypt and return to Nazareth in southern Galilee, near the great caravan trade route.

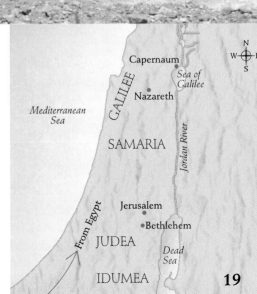

19

"IN MY FATHER'S HOUSE"
LUKE 2:41-52

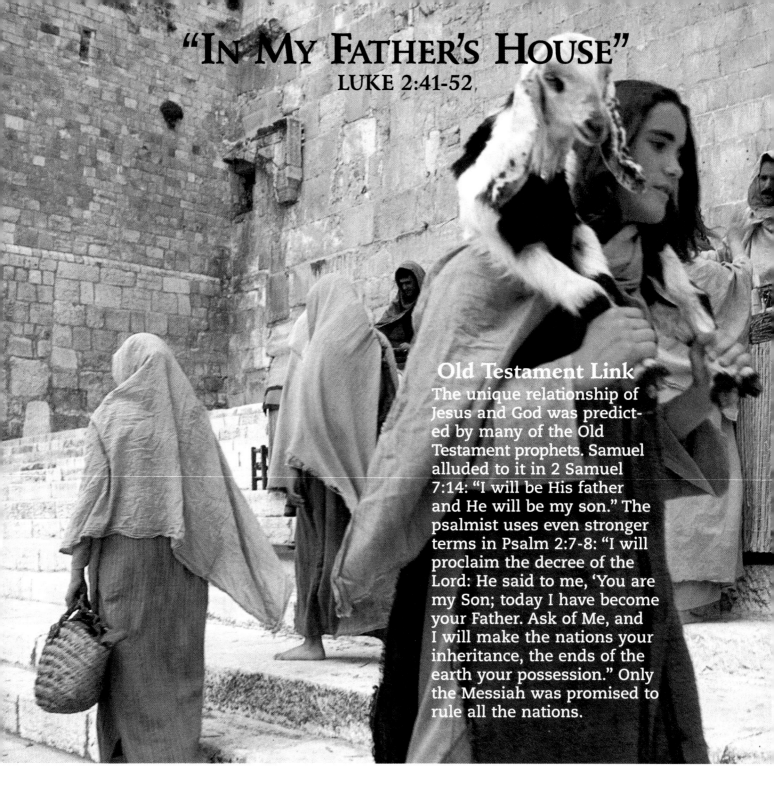

Old Testament Link
The unique relationship of Jesus and God was predicted by many of the Old Testament prophets. Samuel alluded to it in 2 Samuel 7:14: "I will be His father and He will be my son." The psalmist uses even stronger terms in Psalm 2:7-8: "I will proclaim the decree of the Lord: He said to me, 'You are my Son; today I have become your Father. Ask of Me, and I will make the nations your inheritance, the ends of the earth your possession." Only the Messiah was promised to rule all the nations.

Many rituals and holy days fired the imagination of a young Jewish boy in the first century. Children looked forward to Hanukkah, Purim, and the Festival of Tabernacles, when the youngest members of the household would sleep under the stars in a backyard tabernacle, commemorating Israel's 40-year wilderness sojourn.

But nothing could compare with the visits to Jerusalem that every Jewish male made during the three major feasts of Israel: The Festival of Unleavened Bread (Passover), The Festival of Weeks (Pentecost), and The Festival of Shelters (Tabernacles).

As worshippers of all ages approached Jerusalem, the Holy City rose majestically from deep valleys and ravines; a walled city with massive gates and towers. Jesus, now age 12, also traveled to Jerusalem with His parents to attend the Passover feast. After the days of

celebration were complete, the young Jesus chose not to join His family for the journey back to Nazareth.

Remaining behind, Jesus listened to Israel's most learned teachers and elders in the courts of the Temple. His profound questions demonstrated they were not dealing with an ordinary young man, but one who was full of wisdom and knowledge (Luke 2:52). These conversations in all likelihood, began when the

New Testament Fulfillment

Jesus first proclaimed His deity to His parents when they found Him in the Temple. Calling God His Father, Jesus said: "...I had to be in my Father's house" (Luke 2:49). Later it was His unique relationship to God as His Father that led the Jewish elders to understand that He was claiming to be God.

teachers learned Jesus was old enough to be a "Son of the Covenant" (Bar Mitzvah). For the religious leaders, their understanding of Scripture was based on oral traditions passed down from Moses, Joshua, Samuel and the prophets. Over the years these oral traditions became distorted and began to nullify God's Word. In contrast to their current understanding of Scripture, Jesus gave them insights and revelations that had never occurred to them.

Upon finding Him safe in the Temple, Mary began to scold Jesus for the scare He gave the family by not returning. Jesus' response to His mother was the first public assertion of His divinity: "Why are you searching for Me? Didn't you know that I had to be in my Father's house?"

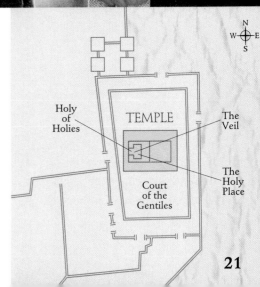

A young Jesus spoke to the elders in the court of His Father's house, the Temple.

THE BAPTISM OF JESUS
MATTHEW 3:13-17

Old Testament Link

Jesus' baptism is linked to two Old Testament ideas: a forerunner announcing the Messiah, and water immersion for purification. Isaiah prophesied that there would be a forerunner of the Messiah, and Malachi said this forerunner would be Elijah (Isaiah 40:3; Malachi 3:1, 4:4-5). Baptism's roots are clearly found in the Old Testament. The word "sanctify" or "consecrate" was understood not only as spiritual cleansing but as physical washing by the Jewish people (Exodus 19:10). Purification was another word used to describe ritual washing (Leviticus 12:5; Numbers 8:7, 31:19). Priests also had to be immersed before assuming their priestly duties (Exodus 29:4, 40:12).

The Jewish people recognized John the Baptist as a prophet sent from God. Even the often petulant Pharisees and Sadducees acknowledged John's calling as a prophet. Some mistook John the Baptist for the Messiah, but he was quick to identify himself as only the forerunner of the Messiah. The Old Testament prophet Malachi said the forerunner would be Elijah, and John's rough-hewn garb was similar to Elijah's. Later in His ministry, Jesus said that John was that promised prophet.

John called for the sons of Israel to prepare for the Kingdom of God and the Messiah by repenting and being baptized.

Why was Jesus baptized? If He was indeed the Messiah and without sin, what reason was there for Him to repent? Scripture declared that Jesus never sinned (2 Corinthians 5:21; Hebrews 4:15, 7:26; 1 John 3:5). John himself questioned Jesus concerning this. "To fulfill all righteousness," was His response.

Perhaps Jesus requested baptism so he could identify completely with sinners. Still another reason might have been that immersion was required of priests before they assumed their duties. One of Jesus' roles was that of High Priest.

But the answer may also lie in the simple routineness and ritual of water immersion. Jewish tradition taught that Mikvah (baptism) was the proper means for spiritual cleansing. Many occasions in everyday life called for immersion in "living waters," including conversion of proselytes, repentance and return from idolatry.

John made it clear, however, that religion was insufficient reason for baptism. There had to be evidence of genuine repentance.

In the Jordan River, John the Baptist proclaimed Jesus to be the Messiah.

New Testament Fulfillment
Jesus declared that John was the greatest of all the prophets: "And if you are willing to accept it, he is the Elijah who was to come" (Matthew 11:14). Jesus, as our High Priest, had to be immersed as He began His priestly ministry (Hebrews 2:17, 3:1, 4:14-15, 5:10).

THE WILDERNESS TEMPTATION
MATTHEW 4:1-11

Old Testament Link

The temptation of Jesus contains elements which reflect the temptation of Adam in the Garden of Eden. Adam's disobedience in the garden signaled the fall, but God's purposes for mankind would not be thwarted (Genesis 3:15). Immediately after pronouncing the curse of the fall, God promised One who would come and, unlike Adam, obey God's Word, and therefore prevail against Satan.

Jesus did not walk into the wilderness after his baptism without a purpose. He knew the temptation set before Him in the barren Judean hills was to complete an ancient and failed mission.

In the Garden of Eden, Adam had failed to withstand Satan's temptation. Thousands of years later, Israel, too was disobedient in the wilderness. If mankind was to have a redeemer, he would have to withstand the schemes of The Adversary.

Tradition places the desolate site of Jesus' test high over Jerico. Weak from fasting, chilled and deprived of any human contact for 40 days, the second Adam faced the tempter.

"If you are the Son of God, tell these stones to become bread," Satan whispered.

"Man does not live on bread alone," Jesus countered, "but on every word that comes from the mouth of God."

Twice more Satan tempted the Messiah to abandon His mission. He transported Jesus to the pinnacle of the Temple, a dizzying 45 stories above the Kidron Valley. Satan asked Jesus to prove His deity by calling upon angels to rescue Him after hurling Himself from the top of the Temple sanctuary.

"Do not put the Lord your God to the test," Jesus answered.

Finally, Satan offered Jesus dominion over the world if the Christ would worship him and end His ministry. He laid out before Christ a vision of all kingdoms of the world.

For the third time Jesus responded with the Word of His Father: "Worship the Lord your God, and serve Him only," effectively banishing Satan.

While Adam's disobedience signaled the fall, Jesus responded with Scripture and resisted. As the second Adam, Jesus obeyed God and remained without sin, and qualified to redeem God's creation.

Jesus was tempted in the wilderness of Judea before returning to His boyhood home of Nazareth.

New Testament Fulfillment

The first man was from the earth; the second, Jesus, was from heaven. In the Judean wilderness, Jesus was tempted three times by Satan to sin. But unlike Adam, Jesus resisted. In His obedience to God, He proved Himself to be the Righteous One who would take upon Himself the judgment that was due to mankind. Thus the apostle Paul wrote: "The first man Adam became a living being; the last Adam, a life-giving spirit" (1 Corinthians 15:45).

FISHERS OF MEN
LUKE 5:1-11

Old Testament Link

Seven hundred years before the calling of the disciples, the prophet Isaiah spoke of a time when the light of God would come upon a people who walked in darkness. This was to take place in the Roman-dominated Galilee (Isaiah 9:1-2). This prophecy found its fulfillment in the ministry of Jesus. This light would not just be for the Gentiles of Galilee; God wanted His light to shine upon all people. The calling of the Jewish fishermen was the first step by which God would bring that light.

The Sea of Galilee is actually a freshwater lake that had offered many fishermen a livelihood through the ages, including at least seven of the disciples.

Many of their days were spent mending their nets; in fact, Andrew was doing just that when Jesus called him as a disciple. Fishermen's nights, however, were spent fishing, when the catch was most plentiful. They drew the fish to their nets with torches made of twigs and vegetable material soaked in oil. Their nets were sometimes hundreds of feet long, ringed with small lead weights.

Thus, Jesus' invitation to the fishermen to become His disciples — fishers of men — was framed with the elements of their daily vocation: He was the light that would draw all men to Himself. His description of the End of the Age, when angels would sort His harvest between those worthy of the Kingdom and those designated for eternal punishment — must have galvanized them. They also had to sort their catch; the unclean (catfish, eel and lamprey) had to be separated from the clean (those fish suitable for Jewish consumption).

When the Lord told Peter to go out to sea and let down his nets for a catch of fish, Peter resisted, telling Jesus he had tried all night with no success.

When Peter eventually obeyed and experienced the astonishing results, he knew this was the Messiah, God in the flesh.

Jesus didn't command His disciples to be fishers of men. Instead, He told them He would *make* them fishers of men. As the disciples were willing to follow Jesus, learn of Him and be yoked to Him, He would transform them into the servants that all history has known them to be.

Fishermen on the Sea of Galilee used nets, often bell-shaped with lead weights around the edges. A net would sink, covering the fish. The fishermen would pull a cord drawing the net around the fish.

New Testament Fulfillment

Peter learned that Jesus of Nazareth was not only a prophet. The haul of fish described in Luke 5 led him to surrender his life, leaving his physical nets permanently to become God's spiritual fisherman. His seas would henceforth be the world and his catch would be the sons of men.

THE FIRST MIRACLE
JOHN 2:1-11

Old Testament Link

God described His relationship with Israel as that of a husband to a wife (Jeremiah 31:31-32; Ezekiel 16:8). God called Israel to be a faithful wife (Jeremiah 3:1-5, 20), but because of her adultery with other gods, He separated himself from her. Even after withholding His blessings, Israel refused to turn back to God. Thus God was forced to issue His certificate of divorce (Jeremiah 3:8). In the midst of her punishment, God called Israel to repent.

Located a few miles from Nazareth, Cana is a small town built on the slope of a hill. Tourists still come to renew their marriage vows at the town where Jesus celebrated a wedding feast. Cana's fame directly relates to the Bible, for here Jesus performed His first miracle.

Mary and her family attended a wedding at Cana. Jesus and His disciples arrived a few days after the ceremonies had begun. In biblical times, the wedding ceremony and reception lasted from seven to 14 days (Genesis 29:27). His presence at the wedding feast so early in His ministry had a certain poignancy. As He watched the newly married couple, He probably noticed the loving gaze that each had for the other. Jesus would never marry nor know the earthly joy of such a union.

He had already grasped His life's mission. His bride would be the Church; all those who would hear His words and believe He was the Messiah would be sent for their eternal salvation. But before His own marriage to the Church, there would be men to teach, blind eyes to open, and sick to heal. There also would be rejection, betrayal, suffering and finally, death.

In Cana that day, His mother's face suddenly caught His attention. The wedding party had run out of wine and Mary trusted Jesus to do something.

Servants filled six stone jars with more than 20 gallons of water each, as Jesus requested. Then one of the servants took the miraculous wine to the master of the banquet who unknowingly said: "You have saved the best till now."

Is there any significance to this first miracle taking place at a wedding? Yes, for marriage is a sacred institution to God; so sacred He refers to believers as His bride and Himself as the bridegroom.

After His baptism and temptation by Satan, Jesus visited Nazareth, Cana and Capernaum before traveling to Jerusalem for Passover.

New Testament Fulfillment

Jesus is the groom who has come for His bride-to-be, the Church (Matthew 9:15). The Bible describes believers of Christ as betrothed to Him; they will celebrate the marriage supper in heaven, when they will be formally married to their husband, the Lord.

THE WOMAN AT THE WELL
JOHN 4:1-42

Old Testament Link

Jesus' reference to water is an allusion to Isaiah 55:1-6, where the prophet spoke of providing water to he who thirsts. In Zechariah 14, the prophet described a thousand-year kingdom when "living waters" would flow out of Jerusalem.

There were no greater outcasts in Jesus' day than the Samaritans. To the Jewish people they represented a hopelessly lost people; half-Jews who worshiped in the wrong place and the wrong way.

When Jesus met a Samaritan woman at Jacob's Well, He made references to this: "You Samaritans worship what you do not know; we worship what we do know, for salvation is from the Jews."

Beginning with Jeroboam, all of the kings of Israel had encouraged idolatry until God could stand it no longer. God allowed the Assyrians to invade and take captive the northern portion of Israel. In time the exiled northern Israelites committed the most grievous of all sins with the Assyrians: intermarriage. Hence, the Samaritans became known as half-breeds, and they succumbed to regular idol worship.

When Jesus came to Samaria, the attitude of the Jewish people had changed little. The apostle John recorded that day's negative prevailing mood towards this land of spiritual compromise: "Now He had to go through Samaria." Normally, a Jewish traveler going from Galilee to Jerusalem would go out of his way, even adding a day to his trip, to avoid setting foot in Samaria.

Jesus, however, took the direct route. He showed no rejection of a woman he came across who had been married five times. Instead, throwing aside all social and religious tradition, Jesus asked the Samaritan woman for a drink. A "religious" discussion ensued wherein the Samaritan woman tried to prove she knew something about current (and future) events. She tried to avoid this One who "told me everything I ever did."

Jesus taught that God is not concerned with how "religious" we are, but rather how genuine our relationship is with Him.

Jacob's Well was probably more than 200 feet deep. It was not spring fed, but collected water from rain and dew.

New Testament Fulfillment

After receiving a cup of water from an outcast Samaritan woman, Jesus for the first time describes the "living water" that He will give to those who follow Him in Spirit and in truth. Later in Jerusalem "Jesus stood and cried out, saying, 'If any man is thirsty, let him come to Me and drink. He who believes in Me, as the Scripture said, "From his innermost being shall flow rivers of living water" (John 7:37-38).

THE SERMON ON THE MOUNT
MATTHEW 5:1-7:23

Old Testament Link
The prophet Jeremiah spoke of a time that would come when God would give His people a new covenant, an agreement written upon their hearts, not on tablets of stone (Jeremiah 31:31-33).

Even in Israel, land of antiquity, the modern world vies jealously for attention. Today, jets roar over the Dead Sea and cars whiz past Canaanite ruins. But there is one place where Jesus spoke that seems little changed since He walked there. In fact, just one hundred yards from the church that rests at the site of the Sermon on the Mount, the confluence of earth, sea and sky still seem to be resonating with the words He spoke there. Perhaps it is the gentle slope of the land upward from the shore of the Galilee and the heavy boughs of thousand-year-old trees fluttering sweetly and effortlessly in the breeze, in perfect harmony with all of creation.

It is not hard to imagine Jesus standing at the water's edge, using the natural acoustics of the hill like an amphitheater to project His voice up to His followers.

His words conveyed a naturalness of thought and expression: "You are the salt of the earth...let your light shine before men...do not give dogs what is sacred." But beneath the prosaic surface of His parables, He struck a subversive note that the Pharisees could not help but hear. For He was telling the crowds that if their righteousness did not exceed the righteousness of the Pharisees and Saducees, they would not enter heaven.

The precepts and beatitudes He articulated were the principles of a new kingdom and a new covenant that superseded the current relationship existing between God and His people.

The dominant message of the Sermon on the Mount is that right theology, philosophy or separation from the world is not as essential as a "right heart." And the right heart requires a "new heart" (Jeremiah 31:31), where a new king would reside.

The Sermon on the Mount was given on a hillside near Capernaum before enormous crowds, and probably lasted several days.

New Testament Fulfillment

In the Sermon on the Mount, Jesus outlined the principles of the Kingdom of God and a new covenant, one based on the Holy Spirit living in their hearts (Hebrews 8:6-13).

CAPERNAUM, A PLACE OF POWER
MATTHEW 8:14-17

Old Testament Link

The prophet Isaiah foretold that the Messiah, the Servant of the Lord, would heal our diseases and remove our infirmities (Isaiah 53:4). This would not fully be experienced until the King returns to reign over His Kingdom, when sin is fully removed. Jesus gave a foretaste of His coming Kingdom when He graciously healed the multitudes.

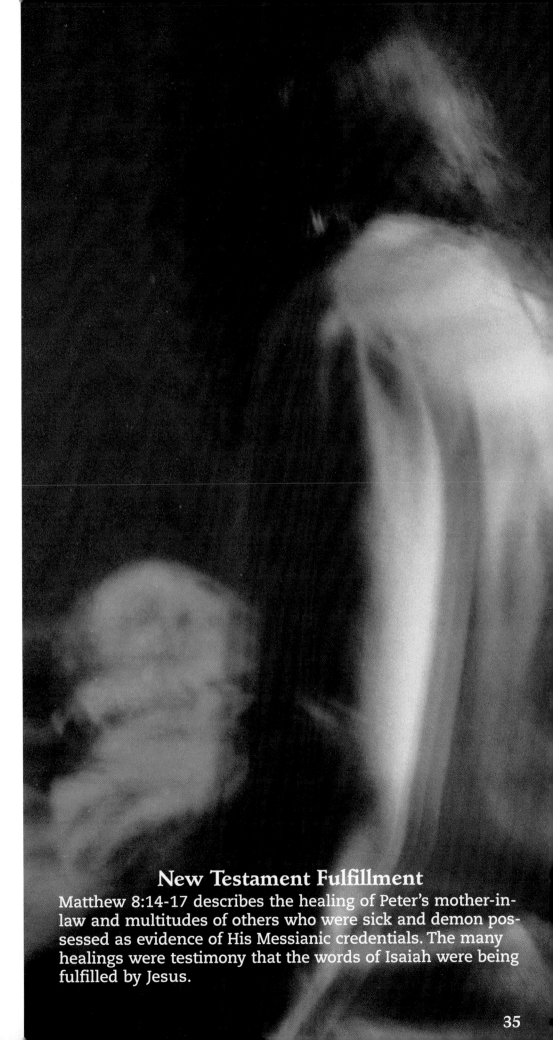

Today, Capernaum never fails to draw archaeologists, pilgrims and tourists. The well-preserved ruins mark the approximate site of a synagogue where Jesus actually taught. But the friezes, columns and benches where worshippers sat, though rich in history, cannot even hint at the excitement of what actually transpired here.

As long as the synagogue stood, worship had been routine. Each Sabbath, the rabbis and sages stood to expound some fine point of Scripture, doubtless referring to a long line of wizened sages before them. This was the first thing they noticed about Jesus: His discourse was not dependent on earlier scholars. Instead, He taught with the authority of God (Matthew 7:29).

One day, as if to validate this authority, He turned to a man in the synagogue who had long been a nuisance to the congregation because of the demon that controlled him. Jesus spoke directly to the evil spirit: "'Come out of him!' The evil spirit shook the man violently and came out of him with a shriek." (Mark 1:25-26).

Leaving the synagogue, Jesus went to the home of His disciple, Peter. Inside lay Peter's mother-in-law, sick with fever. Under rabbinical law, it was forbidden to touch people who were with fever. To do so was to cause oneself to be defiled. With the same authority that He had called the demon out of the man in the synagogue, He instantly healed Peter's mother-in-law with the slightest touch.

The news of these miracles was impossible to ignore. By sunset, Peter's house in Capernaum was overwhelmed with the sick and demon-possessed: "The whole town gathered at the door…" (Mark. 1:33).

Situated on the Sea of Galilee, Capernaum was a wealthy city due to fishing and trade. A cultural melting pot, the city was influenced by Greek and Roman customs, dress, architecture and politics.

New Testament Fulfillment

Matthew 8:14-17 describes the healing of Peter's mother-in-law and multitudes of others who were sick and demon possessed as evidence of His Messianic credentials. The many healings were testimony that the words of Isaiah were being fulfilled by Jesus.

TOUCHING A LEPER
LUKE 5:12-14

Old Testament Link

The Mosaic Law gave guidelines for the isolation and ostracism of lepers, but nothing was indicated for the cure of leprosy. Isaiah prophesied that the Messiah would carry others' "infirmities" and "sorrows" (Isaiah 53:4), metaphors for leprosy. The Talmud also connected the healing of leprosy with the Messiah, even going so far as to name Him "the leprous," picturing Him "as seated in the entrance to Rome, surrounded by and relieving all misery and disease in fulfillment of Isaiah 53:4." The Jewish people of Jesus' day understood that the healing of leprosy was possible only through God.

In terms of physical and social defilement, nothing ranked worse in Israel than leprosy. Though many religious leaders thought blindness, deafness and palsy were the result of sin, leprosy was believed to be God's direct punishment for special sins.

The debilitating disease typically began on the eyelids as tiny specks, then spread to the palms of the hand and the rest of the body. Through a steady deterioration, the victim could eventually suffer dam-age to his underlying tissues, organs and bones. There was no cure.

The leper could speak to no one, nor could others exchange a greeting with him for fear of becoming unclean themselves. He had to keep a distance of six feet — one hundred feet in wind — between himself and others while announcing his presence with the cry "unclean, unclean."

When Jesus entered into a conversation with a leper in one of the villages along the Sea of Galilee, He violated social custom by talking to him. More surprising, He then touched the leper to theoretically (not practically) risk contamination. "Filled with compassion, Jesus reached out his hand and touched the man" (Mark 1:41). Jesus made a point to touch the man first, and then heal him. One must understand that from the time the Chief Priest in the Temple had pronounced this leper unclean, perhaps half his lifetime ago, this unfortunate man ha

New Testament Fulfillment
One of the most convincing proofs of the deity of the Messiah was his healings of those afflicted with leprosy (Luke 5:12-14; 17:11-19).

gone without any human touch. Until Jesus. His actions probably shocked the onlookers, including His disciples.

For a moment, just before the leper threw his face in the dirt, begging: "Lord, if you are willing, make me clean," he must have met Jesus' eyes. And later, like the woman caught in adultery, He must have felt the compassion flowing from Him. In His three words: "I am willing," the leper heard what the woman would soon hear: "neither do I condemn you."

The leper's cleansing would stand as a testimony to Israel of God's power and presence. The hand of the Messiah broke through this leper's shell of loneliness and communicated love in a way that reinforced His words of healing.

By the Sea of Galilee, a man with leprosy approached Jesus and asked to be healed.

EATING WITH THE SINNERS
MATTHEW 9:9-13, 36

Old Testament Link
The prophet Ezekiel had indicted the spiritual leaders for their lack of concern and care for their charges, the children of Israel. Instead of teaching and loving them, they acted like wayward shepherds who scattered the sheep through their harsh domination. But the Lord Himself promised that He would search and find His lost sheep (Ezekiel 34:1-5, 11-16).

The Jewish people wanted nothing to do with Matthew in Jesus' time. He was a publican, one whom the occupying Romans had hired to gather tax monies. In order to earn a living, publicans usually inflated the tolls and taxes they collected, sometimes to unreasonable proportions. Matthew collected tolls on the road between Acco and Damascus and also probably from fishermen working on the Sea of Galilee.

Publicans like Matthew were despised for charging above the actual tolls. They were hated because they were traitors to their people — giving the hard earned money of their countrymen to the Roman government with its figurehead king, Herod.

The Jewish people of Jesus' day considered a publican's money so unclean they refused to defile themselves by receiving even the change from their payment. The Jewish establishment prohibited publicans from testifying in court, and they were not allowed to tithe money to the Temple. It was understood that no self-respecting Jew would associate with them.

Jesus, however, called Matthew to follow Him as one of His disciples. Later Jesus ate a meal with Matthew and other tax collectors. Seeing this the Pharisees were furious. They believed that Matthew and his friends were beyond God's forgiveness.

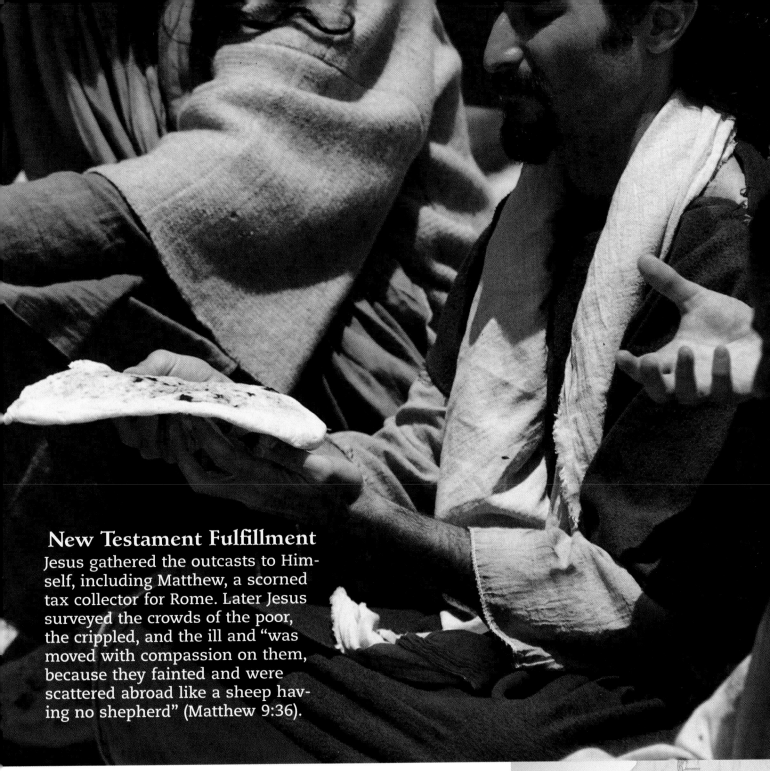

New Testament Fulfillment

Jesus gathered the outcasts to Himself, including Matthew, a scorned tax collector for Rome. Later Jesus surveyed the crowds of the poor, the crippled, and the ill and "was moved with compassion on them, because they fainted and were scattered abroad like a sheep having no shepherd" (Matthew 9:36).

Though no Pharisee or scribe of the Mosaic Law would set foot in Matthew's house, Jesus did. The rabbi from Galilee not only met and ate with Matthew and other tax collectors, but also probably with other outcasts of Pharisaic society.

When the Pharisees asked how Jesus could socialize with "tax collectors and sinners," He answered that He came to heal the sick, not the healthy. In their veneration of the oral law which they revered as coming down the centuries from Moses, the Pharisees had neglected the weightier aspects of the Law — justice and mercy.

Walking on a road near Capernaum, Jesus saw Matthew sitting at his tax collection booth and said: "follow me."

HEALING OF THE LAME
JOHN 5:1-15

Old Testament Link

The prophets Isaiah and Zephaniah spoke of the Messiah as one who would heal the lame (Isaiah 33:23; Zephaniah 3:14). In describing the coming kingdom, Isaiah said that the blind would see and that the lame would leap (Isaiah 35:5-6). Jesus gave evidence that He was the promised Messiah with these signs.

Jesus' presence had the effect of focusing a light of truth on any individual or situation. Such a light shone brightly at the Pool of Bethesda, located near the Sheep Gate of Jerusalem's fortified wall. Here Jesus encountered a man who was crippled for 38 years waiting for a chance to enter the pool and be healed.

Today, we are fairly certain that the occasional stirring of the pool's water was nothing more than the chemical reaction of iron, carbonic acid, and other gases "moving" the waters. At that time, the water's movement was thought to be the visitation of angels and thus proof of the pool's "healing" power.

"Do you want to get well?" Jesus asked the man. The words of the Messiah were a divining rod of truth. Obviously, the man, crippled and laying on one of the pool's terraces, would have no other reason to be there. Yet, the rabbi's question probed the depths of the man's heart.

Perhaps this man had become a chronic fixture at the pool, complaining about the unfairness of life. Or being disabled for so long, he might have simply given up hope. Whatever the reason, he did not answer Jesus directly. His response sounded more like an excuse: "I have no one to help me into the pool when the water is stirred. While I am trying to get in, someone else goes down ahead of me."

"Then Jesus said to him, 'Get up! Pick up your mat and walk."

The man rose at once: "He picked up his mat and walked."

Jesus revealed the lame man's innermost aspirations by asking, "Do you want to get well?" Likewise, from the Pharisees He also exposed their hidden thoughts. They refused to accept His power was from God. Instead, they persecuted Him for healing on the Sabbath.

At the pool of Bethesda, inside the city near the Sheep Gate, Jesus came upon a man who had been crippled for 38 years.

New Testament Fulfillment

The disciples of John the Baptist were sent by him to ask Jesus if He really was the promised Messiah. His response was to cite the promise of the prophets concerning the healing of the lame and giving sight to the blind (Matthew 11:4-5; Luke 14:13-14).

WHEAT AND THE SABBATH
MATTHEW 12:1-13

Old Testament Link

The Sabbath was a reminder to Israel that God would provide for them. This day of physical rest foreshadowed the grace of God, who would provide salvation and spiritual rest for His people. The Sabbath was God's sign, setting His people apart from all the nations (Exodus 31:12-17).

Noticing the disciples walking through a field on the Sabbath, picking and eating grain, the Pharisees accused them of breaking the Sabbath. Jesus defended their actions by reminding the Pharisees of King David who, fleeing from Saul, ate the showbread.

His defense, though brilliant, seemed almost irrelevant to the Pharisees. Over the centuries, ever fearful that Israel would break God's commandments, the rabbis and scribes established 39 general categories of actions forbidden on the Sabbath. These laws acted as a "fence" around the Mosaic Law. Every one of God's commandments was extrapolated and applied to every conceivable domestic, vocational and intellectual aspect of life from the practical to the hypothetical. When this oral law was finally collected and recorded in medieval times, these hundred upon hundreds of ancillary laws became known as the Talmud, or the Code of Jewish Law.

The inspiration for such scrupulous legalism might have been well-intended at first. But by Jesus' day, the laws *around* the Law obscured the mercy of God.

Jesus entered a synagogue and healed on the Sabbath to illustrate that mercy was more important than Sabbath rules. Hoping to silence Him, the Pharisees brought Him a man afflicted with a withered arm. Since his sickness was not life-threatening, they reasoned Jesus did not need to heal on the Sabbath. He pointed out that the Pharisees themselves made allowance for rescuing an animal on the Sabbath. How much more valuable to God, He reasoned, was the wholeness of a man.

Jesus commanded the man to stretch out his shrunken arm, and the man responded, manifesting the Lord's healing.

Jesus castigated his critics for their hardness of heart. They decided He was a false prophet.

The farming areas of Israel resemble the wheat fields Jesus most likely walked through on the Sabbath.

New Testament Fulfillment

Jesus declared that by virtue of His deity He was greater than the Temple and thus the Sabbath (Matthew 12:6). The work of Jesus and our rest in His work is a fulfillment of the Sabbath concept (Hebrews 4:9-10).

BLINDED TO THE LIGHT
JOHN 9:1-39

Old Testament Link

"Arise, shine, for your light has come, and the glory of the Lord rises upon you. See, darkness covers the earth and thick darkness is over the peoples, but the Lord rises upon you and his glory appears over you. Nations will come to your light, and kings to the brightness of your dawn" (Isaiah 60:1-3). The prophet Isaiah spoke of a time when God's light would come to Israel and that light would be the glory of the Lord. He declared that all nations would come to this light. Two thousand years ago, Jesus came to the land of Israel and fulfilled this prophecy.

Prevalent sunshine makes Israel today a major fruit supplier of Europe, and it also was the case in Jesus' day. One man born blind had not known the joy of this sunshine. Moreover, he and his family had lived with the stigma that God's light did not shine on them because of sin. Like those with leprosy, men with blindness were thought to have committed some special sin.

Even the disciples believed this, for they asked Jesus: "Rabbi, who sinned, this man or his parents, that he was born blind?" Jesus told His disciples that neither the sin of this blind man nor of his parents had caused his blindness, but rather he was blind so that the work of God might be displayed through him.

Jesus then declared that He was the light of the world. Jesus applied clay and spittle to the man's eyes and sent him to wash in the Pool of Siloam, where his vision was immediately granted.

The very first words recorded in the Scripture was God's declaration "Let there be light." Now once again God in the person of the Messiah declared: "I am the light of the world." But instead of accepting the testimony of the blind man, the Pharisees sought to prove that the man was not really blind to begin with. How the Pharisees responded to the one who brought light into the world determined their eternal destinies.

New Testament Fulfillment

Jesus said: "I am the light of the World" (John 9:5). The context for this statement was the gift of sight to the man who was born blind. The religious leaders thought that the light of God came through their religious tradition, but real light — the light that lights men souls — comes from the person of Jesus.

The Pharisees' ultimate rejection of Jesus could have been different. They could have simply asked God for discernment: "Is Jesus indeed from God?" Or they could have searched the Scriptures to determine if His actions contradicted the Word. Instead, the Pharisees became defensive and protective. Only a few religious men, including Nicodemus and Joseph of Arimathea, apparently chose to meet Jesus with an open, though apprehensive, mind.

After the Pharisees had completed their investigation of this miracle, Jesus summed up the entire episode: "For judgment I have come into this world, so that the blind will see and those who see will become blind."

The Pool of Siloam was built by King Hezekiah. A tunnel was constructed to bring water from a spring outside the city walls, so the people could always have water during a siege or attack.

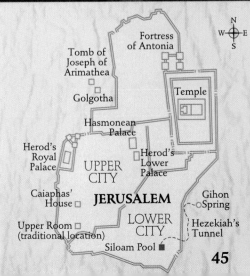

45

A ROMAN SOLDIER'S GREAT FAITH
LUKE 7:1-10

Old Testament Link

Moses spoke prophetically of Israel's future in Deuteronomy 32, predicting God's faithfulness and Israel's disobedience. God said a time woul come when Israel would be made jealous and envious by a people whom they didn't even consider a people (Deuteronomy 32:21). Isaiah and Hosea also saw a picture of a declining faith in Israel's future (Isaiah 65:1; Hosea 2:23)

In Capernaum, a Roman officer approached Jesus requesting that He heal his servant. As a centurion, the commander of a hundred Roman soldiers, he should have been despised by the Jews for being both a Gentile and a leader of the Roman force occupying Judea. Instead, the Jewish community respected and even loved this Roman soldier, who "built our synagogue."

Perhaps the people of Capernaum were not financially able to build their own place of worship and the generosity of this centurion enabled them to have one. In light of Rome's oppressive hand on the community, the kindness of this soldier was comforting and generous. Thus some of the Jewish elders said to Jesus: "This man deserves to have you [heal his servant]."

The servant was probably born in the centurion's household and was highly regarded; this could explain the soldier's concern for his well-being. The compassion of this Roman officer for a slave who had no legal rights is even more remarkable when the fact that Roman military leaders tended to be promoted based upon their cruelty is considered.

When the centurion spoke to Jesus, he demonstrated incredible faith. Instead of asking that Jesus come to his servant, he asked Jesus to only "say the word, and my servant will be healed."

The centurion's request related to his understanding of the Roman military system. All authority belonged to the emperor, who in turn delegated authority to his generals and administrators. When the centurion spoke, it was with the authority of the emperor. The centurion believed that Jesus wielded such spiritual authority.

Jesus marveled at the faith of this Gentile: "I tell you, I have not found such great faith in Israel."

Roman columns still stand in what remains of Capernaum.

New Testament Fulfillment

Before healing a Roman centurion's servant, Jesus declared the soldier's faith to be "great," and superior to anything He had found in all of Israel. Thus Jesus documented the prophets' declarations that the Jewish nation would lack faith. The event marked the beginning of many nations and peoples turning to the God of Israel (Luke 7:9).

CALMING THE STORM
MATTHEW 8:23-27

Old Testament Link
The Old Testament repeatedly describes God as the One who controls and calms the seas; both Job and David in the psalms draw poetic pictures of God subduing forceful waters (Job 38:8-11; Psalm 65:5-7). "You rule over the surging sea; When its waves mount up, you still them" (Psalm 89:9).

The ministry of Jesus was no longer confined to just His 12 disciples. His ability to heal and speak authoritatively about the world to come drew crowds wherever He went. Already He had healed a man with leprosy, a sure sign of divine visitation, healed the sick, and uttered the sublime truths of the Sermon on the Mount.

His teachings, His miracles and His good works inspired an outpouring of passionate vows from eyewitnesses. A Jewish teacher of the law, for instance, was willing to risk all he had by stepping out of the crowd and pledging his allegiance publicly to the Messiah. "Teacher," he cried, "I will follow you wherever you go."

His ministry was in full flower. He had healed Peter's sick mother-in-law, preached to the crowds and had driven out spirits from the demon-possessed. He instructed the disciples to set sail for the other side of the sea and then fell asleep.

Located 680 feet below sea level the Sea of Galilee is vulnerable to violent drafts that sometimes rush down the steep mountain passes to the normally placid lake. Such winds can create waves 20 feet high. That night the storm raged so violently that even the seasoned fishermen of Galilee were frightened. Understandably, the disciples feared for their lives and they awoke Jesus, accusing Him of not caring.

New Testament Fulfillment

One of many pieces of evidence that Jesus was the promised Messiah was His power over nature. "He replied, 'You of little faith, why are you so afraid?' Then He got up and rebuked the winds and the waves, and it was completely calm. And the men marveled, saying, 'What kind of a man is this? Even the winds and the waves obey Him!'" (Matthew 8:26-27).

Awakened by the terrified disciples, Jesus rebuked them: "You of little faith…" His criticism may have reflected His disillusionment at their apparent ignorance of His identity as the Lord of Nature.

Rising in the boat, He spoke directly to the wind and waves: "Quiet, be still" (Mark 4:39). The wind died and the lake "was completely calm."

Demons had fled at His word; sickness had vanished with only His touch and now, the wind and the sea obeyed His voice. That night those closest to Him, His disciples, looked on in awe at what they had witnessed: "What kind of man is this?"

In early evening, a boat large enough to hold Jesus and His 12 disciples, was crossing the Sea of Galilee (a body of water 13 miles long, 7 miles wide and 150 feet deep) when a violent storm developed.

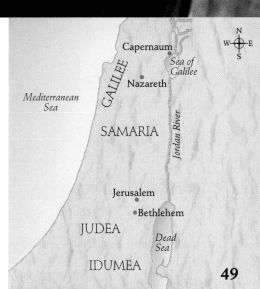

FEEDING OF THE 5000
JOHN 6:1-15

Old Testament Link

In the wilderness, God provided bread (manna) for the wandering Israelites — about three million people who had fled Egypt. Every day manna fell from heaven (Exodus 16:31) and provided sustenance for the children of Israel. When they entered the promised land after 40 years, the manna ceased to fall.

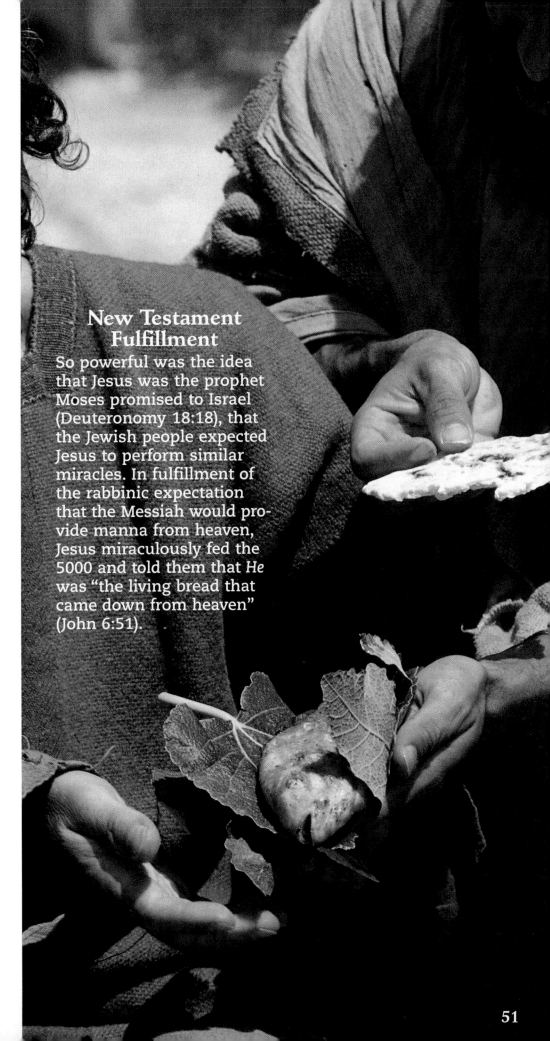

After months of growing popularity, Jesus desired to withdraw from the masses for several reasons. John the Baptist had been beheaded by the Romans who feared his influence. Jesus may have felt that the loss of John would cause people to make Him king for only emotional reasons. Also, the disciples needed rest. Most important, He needed to teach the disciples undisturbed by crowds.

Jesus left Capernaum by boat, seeking to slip away unnoticed across the Sea of Galilee. But the people followed Him on foot and were waiting for Him when He got ashore. The gospels report that 5000 men were present in the grass as Jesus began to teach. Women and children were also present (Matthew 14:21), increasing the figure to at least 10,000 people. They needed to eat, and the disciples needed a lesson.

"Where shall we buy bread for these people to eat?" Jesus asked Philip (John 6:5). This question was posed to test Philip's faith. He knew that they were far from any village and lacked the money to feed so large a crowd. Jesus took five barley loaves (the cheapest of grains) and two fish and prayed, thanking God for His provision.

The miracle was subtle; the food multiplied in quantity to feed all present imperceptibly. This was an unforgettable lesson in faith for the disciples. The Lord's teaching, however, was not imperceptible. Many times in the future the disciples would be responsible for feeding those who needed spiritual food. Instead of thinking of this ministry as their own, they were to thank God, offer what they had to Him, and He would multiply their resources to satisfy the multitudes.

The miracle of the loaves and fishes convinced many that Jesus was the Messiah. But Jesus, perceiving that the mass' desire was for a temporal king, withdrew further into the hills.

Jesus fed the multitude on a hillside near the Sea of Galilee at Bethsaida-Julias.

New Testament Fulfillment

So powerful was the idea that Jesus was the prophet Moses promised to Israel (Deuteronomy 18:18), that the Jewish people expected Jesus to perform similar miracles. In fulfillment of the rabbinic expectation that the Messiah would provide manna from heaven, Jesus miraculously fed the 5000 and told them that *He* was "the living bread that came down from heaven" (John 6:51).

FREEING A DEMON-POSSESSED MAN
MARK 5:1-20

Old Testament Link

The Old Testament described demons as fallen servants of God. The evil spirit that troubled King Saul was sent by the Lord (1 Samuel 16:14), and the Lord sen an evil spirit to deceive Ahab (1 Kings 22:20-23). Men who would not serve God were the most vulnerable to being influenced by these fallen angels.

The Pharisees didn't deny that Jesus could do miracles. They simply attributed them to the powers of Satan. Yet Jesus continued to demonstrate the Kingdom of God. He healed a blind and dumb man, taught the people in parables and He calmed a violent storm while crossing the Sea of Galilee.

But when He arrived, all was not calm.

Living in the region of the Gadarenes was a demon-possessed man who met Jesus as His feet touched land. So violent was the sway these evil spirits held over the man that the townspeople had to restrain him with chains, which he continually broke.

As the possessed man rampaged toward Jesus, the Messiah called the demons out of him. "When he saw Jesus from a distance, he ran and fell on his knees in front of him. He shouted at the top of his voice, 'What do you want with me Jesus, Son of the most High God?"

The demons not only recognized Jesus for who He was but they were also aware of God's future plans for them, as they asked through the man: "Have you come here to torture us before the appointed time?" (Matthew 8:29). Speaking directly to the demons, Jesus asked what their name was. "My name is Legion," he replied. "For we are many." (A possible reference to a Roman legion which consisted of 3000-6000 men.)

Jesus gave the demons permission to enter a herd of swine grazing nearby. Immediately, the 2000 swine hurled themselves over the steep bank into the sea and drowned.

As Jesus prepared to leave, the demon-possessed man, now in his right mind, begged to go with Him. Jesus declined, instructing him to remain as a testimony to the mercy of God.

After crossing the Sea of Galilee, Jesus landed in Gadarenes. Here He sent demons out of a man into a herd of swine that plunged over this hill and ran into the sea.

New Testament Fulfillment

Demons are described in the New Testament as spiritual beings who enact Satan's purposes (Matthew 12:26). They later are described as beings who attempt to deceive God's people (Ephesians 6:12). They will be judged and their final doom will be in the eternal fire (Jude 6; 2 Peter 2:4, Matthew 25:41).

Healing The Blind And The Mute
MATTHEW 9:27-33

Old Testament Link

Throughout the Old Testament, God is spoken of as a healer of mankind's ills. The prophet Isaiah revealed God's declaration that when the Messiah came: "Then will the eyes of the blind be opened and the ears of the deaf unstopped" (Isaiah 35:5).

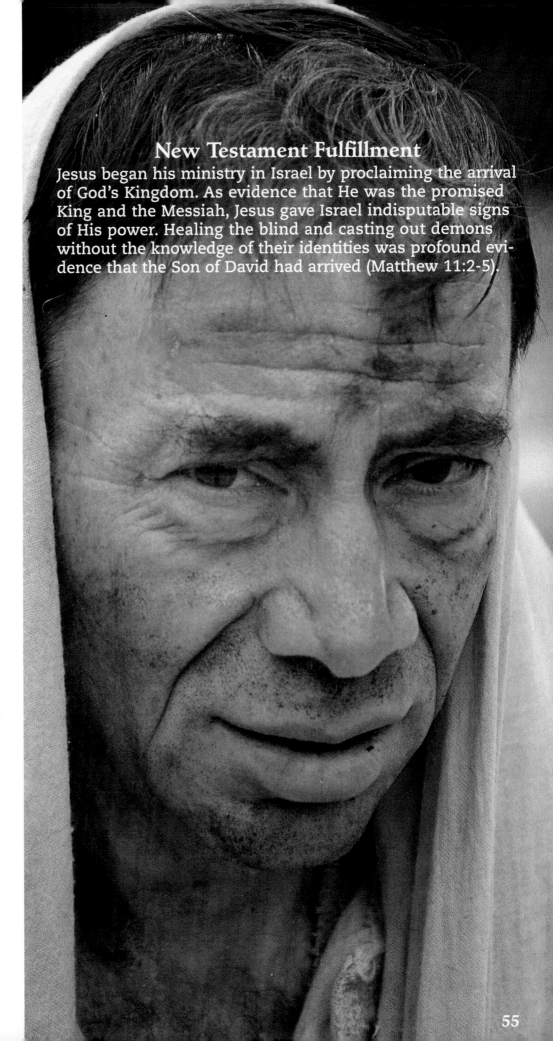

Matthew records five notable miracles in Jesus' hometown of Capernaum. During one remarkable day of ministry, Jesus first healed a paralytic and then brought total health to a woman who suffered for 12 years from a bleeding disorder — she was healed merely by touching the fringes of His prayer shawl. Next He entered the house of a synagogue official and raised the man's daughter from death. Then two blind men crying out His Messianic title, "Son of David," were given sight.

Each of these miracles could individually authenticate the Messianic authenticity of Jesus. But His involvement in a special case, famous among the itinerant Jewish exorcists, drew special attention. These miracle-working rabbis could burn incense and chant mysterious incantations all day to no avail; it was impossible for them to cast the demon out of one born mute. The exorcist had to be able to establish a conversation with the demon through the host in order to know its identity and call it out. Since the mute could not talk, the demon was unable to speak through him, identify itself and be cast out. Only the Son of God could cast out a demon from a host so afflicted.

Without any type of incantation or any knowledge of the demon's identity, Jesus cast out the demon simply by the authority of His word. Suddenly, for the first time in his life, the mute was talking. The crowd was stunned. "Nothing like this has ever been seen in Israel."

On this remarkable day, many in Israel came to believe as they witnessed the miracles of God. The Pharisees, however, rejected the miracles by attributing the work of Jesus to the power of Satan.

The people of Israel were overwhelmed by the Divine One in their midst.

As Jesus left the home where He raised a dead girl, two blind men from Capernaum followed Him.

New Testament Fulfillment

Jesus began his ministry in Israel by proclaiming the arrival of God's Kingdom. As evidence that He was the promised King and the Messiah, Jesus gave Israel indisputable signs of His power. Healing the blind and casting out demons without the knowledge of their identities was profound evidence that the Son of David had arrived (Matthew 11:2-5).

Walking On Water
MATTHEW 14:24-33

Old Testament Link

A psalmist wrote that the Lord "makes winds his messengers, flames of fire his servants" (Psalm 104:4). Augur wrote that the one who gathered the wind in His fists had a son (Proverbs 30:4). The "Anointed One" of Psalm 2 is identified as "the Son." The Old Testament writers believed that the promised Son would have the powers of nature at His disposal.

As the creator of all that existed on the earth, the Messiah could coax a sermon as easily from a lily on a Galilean hillside as from a blazing sunset over the mountains of Judea. But one lesson He taught was so terrifying that the disciples certainly would have preferred their education on a less dynamic campus!

Though they had just seen Jesus miraculously feed the 5000, their faith was not strong. Scripture says that "they had not understood about the loaves; their hearts were hardened" (Mark 6:52). Purposefully, Jesus sent the disciples to their boat intending for them to sail for the other side of the Sea of Galilee. Not long after launching out, with the vessel probably three to four miles from shore, a terrible storm surfaced.

Jesus came to them in the fourth watch, between 3 and 6 a.m., which meant the disciples probably had been battling the storm for about eight hours.

Tired and fearful, they were stunned at the sight: their Master was walking across the waters of Galilee!

Instead of rejoicing at the sight of Jesus coming to them on the water, they became even more frightened.

Peter, however, demonstrated remarkable faith when he climbed out of the boat and advanced toward Jesus on the water. Peter's first steps were safe, but soon he became overwhelmed by the fury all around him. Sinking, his cries of despair were met instantly as Jesus rescued him.

Through this miracle, Jesus taught that a walk like Peter's, initiated by faith, must continue by faith. The disciples were to continue looking at Jesus during every adversity. Even in the bleakest storms, though He tarries, though He remains for a while beyond their sight, He is still there.

Around four o'clock in the morning, Jesus came to the disciples walking on the Sea of Galilee.

New Testament Fulfillment

Jesus said the Son of Man is the one who descended from heaven (John 3:13), even as Augur described Him in Proverbs 30:4. This same Son further proved His credentials by walking on water.

ON THIS ROCK
I WILL BUILD MY CHURCH
MATTHEW 16:18-19

Old Testament Link

God called Abraham out of Ur of the Chaldees. Later, He would call the Jewish nation to Himself as His own, special and holy possession (Deuteronomy 7:6-8); chosen and set apart. Just so, He would later, in the New Testament, call the Church out from the world, as a special possession for Himself.

Appearances can be deceiving. Who would believe that the mighty Jordan and the vast Sea of Galilee, which bring life to the sunbaked Land of Israel, begin their flow on the snowy caps of Mount Hermon. Melting snow trickles down its slopes, winds its way through underground tributaries and collects at one of the most beautiful spots on earth, the Banias at Caesarea Phillipi.

It was here that Peter made his stunning confession of faith, identifying Jesus not only as the Messiah but as "the Son of the living God." It is particularly ironic that Peter should make his confession amid a verdant grove blooming with every variety of tree, wild bush, flower and bubbling fountain. The splendor of Banias was corrupt to the core. Thousands of years earlier it had been a Canaanite sanctuary for the worship of Baal. By the time Jesus sojourned there it was still a pagan stronghold; a center of Greco-Roman civilization. In fact, the Greeks had substituted a shrine to their god, Pan, in place of the older one celebrating Baal.

Jesus' response to Peter's confession is significant when one considers where He made it — Banias, the beautiful but demonic garden of idol worship. As He uttered the decisive: "And I tell you that you are Peter, and on this rock I will build my church, and the gates of Hades will not overcome it," He may have gestured toward the pagan shrine of Pan that stood in front of the entrance to an underground cavern. Today in Banias, amidst nature's finery, the shrine to Pan still stands. But compared to the Church and the body of believers that Jesus predicted He would build, it is merely a dusty footnote from antiquities.

Caesarea Phillipi was located several miles north of the Sea of Galilee in the territory of Tetrarch Phillip.

New Testament Fulfillment

Matthew 16 contains the first reference to the Church, or *ecclesia* (called-out ones), in the New Testament. Addressing the disciples in response to Peter's confession that He is the Son of the living God, Jesus stated that on that rock (Peter's confession) He would build His Church. Like Israel, called by God to be separate, so Jesus calls the Church to be separate from the world (Titus 2:14), His possession, His bride.

THE TRANSFIGURATION OF JESUS
LUKE 9:28-36

Old Testament Link

The prophet Zechariah declared that when the Messiah came to establish his Kingdom, all the nations would celebrate the Festival of Tabernacles (Zechariah 14:16). The Messiah would bring a glorious light to Israel so that the Gentiles would come and experience the glory of the Lord.

The disciples had seen their rabbi feed 5000 people, heal the blind and raise the dead. In their minds, His kingdom was an imminent reality. Why then was He telling them that His next move was to go to Jerusalem and die?

The concept of a suffering Messiah was so discouraging to the disciples, Jesus had to take them on a journey far away to explain His mission undisturbed.

He took three disciples — Peter, James and John — to Mount Hermon, a series of snow-capped peaks in the north. Once He had drawn them away to this mountain retreat, He spent time explaining God's great plan for the salvation of the world.

Withdrawing from the three to pray to the Father, He was suddenly transfigured. The Scripture states: "His face shone like the sun, and his clothes became as white as the light. Just then there appeared before them Moses and Elijah, talking with Jesus" (Matthew 17:2-3).

For Jesus, who had left His Father, the Transfiguration, in a moment, revealed His original glory. Yet the talk between the Messiah, Elijah and Moses was of what lay before Him: "His departure" from Calvary (Luke 9:31).

Peter was convinced he was witnessing the beginning of the great Messianic Kingdom. He linked this event to the celebration of the Festival of Tabernacles. An excited Peter suggested to Jesus that three tabernacles be built: "one for you, one for Moses and one for Elijah."

The Transfiguration also revealed one of the deepest mysteries of God: the translation of believers from earth to heaven. Paul wrote: "We will not all sleep [die] but we will all be changed — in a flash, in the twinkling of an eye" (1 Corinthians 15:51-52). Thus every believer in the Messiah will one day share in the same transfigured glory that Jesus experienced on Mount Hermon.

High above the land, the Mount of Transfiguration (Mount Hermon) can be seen from great distances.

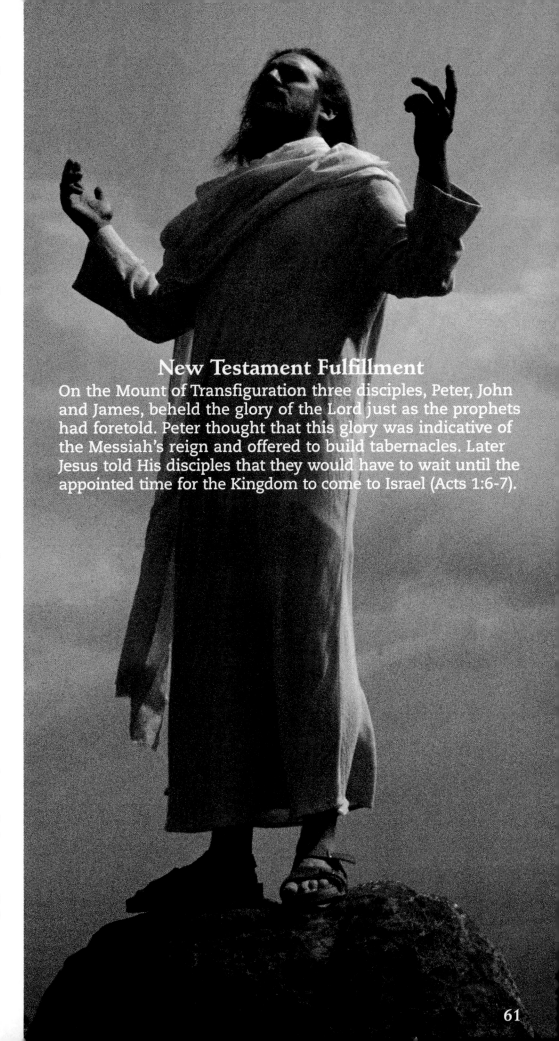

New Testament Fulfillment

On the Mount of Transfiguration three disciples, Peter, John and James, beheld the glory of the Lord just as the prophets had foretold. Peter thought that this glory was indicative of the Messiah's reign and offered to build tabernacles. Later Jesus told His disciples that they would have to wait until the appointed time for the Kingdom to come to Israel (Acts 1:6-7).

AT THE HOME OF MARY AND MARTHA
LUKE 10:38-41

Old Testament Link
Isaiah was overwhelmed at the sight of the Lord in His vision and cried out: "Woe to me...I am ruined!" (Isaiah 6:5). According to tradition, to see the Lord in the flesh was a flirtation with death. This too was the response of Manoah, Samson's father (Judges 13:22). In both of these examples the response to a vision of God was worship and fear.

Anticipating bitter rejection in Jerusalem, Jesus found a moment of acceptance and respect at Mary and Martha's home. Their house in Bethany, a few miles outside of Jerusalem, was probably where Jesus stayed for the first few days of the Festival of Tabernacles before going up to the Temple.

In the courtyard of their home was the tabernacle, a sort of open-air shelter covered over with leafy tree branches. These homemade shelters were to commemorate the Israelite's 40-year exodus from Egypt (Leviticus 23:43).

That was where Jesus sat as Martha and Mary ran between the house and the tabernacle to serve Him. Martha had prepared an elaborate meal, but her sister, Mary, preferred simply sitting entranced at Jesus' feet. It wasn't long before Martha's frustration boiled over.

"Lord, don't you care that my sister has left me to do the work by myself? Tell her to help me!" (Luke 10:40).

Martha was so sure that Jesus would side with her in her complaint against Mary that she demanded He rebuke her sister. The Lord's response must have taken her by surprise.

"Martha, Martha," the Lord answered, "you are worried and upset about many things, but only one thing is needed. Mary has chosen what is better, and it will not be taken away from her."

New Testament Fulfillment

Contrasted with the encounters of the Lord by Isaiah and Manoah was the encounter with Mary and Martha. The glory and awesome power of the Lord was now veiled, but not so much that Mary did not recognize the beauty and wonder of His grace and love (Luke 10:39).

His gentle rebuke speaks volumes. The repetition of her name, "Martha, Martha" belies His affection for her, just as He repeated His disciple's name "Peter, Peter" in tender admonition.

His statement, "only one thing is needed," might refer to the many dishes Martha had prepared and that only one simple dish was necessary.

Finally, Jesus defends Mary. Fellowship with Him was to be valued above the mere preparation for a meal, activity or special celebration.

Jesus was teaching and traveling throughout Galilee. He returned to Jerusalem for the Festival of Tabernacles. While there, He visited his friends Mary and Martha in the village of Bethany located on the slope of the Mount of Olives.

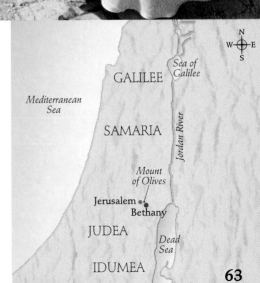

Old Testament Link

God commanded Jewish men to be present three times a year in the Temple: on Passover, Shavuout (Pentecost) and the Festival of Tabernacles (Deuteronomy 16:16). By this command God was setting the stage for the sudden and dramatic appearance of the Messiah at His Temple. The prophet Malachi spoke of a time when the Lord would suddenly appear in the Temple (Malachi 3:1).

From the height of glory on the Mount of the Transfiguration, Jesus descended, resolute, to face the rejection and death that awaited Him in Jerusalem. In the remaining six days of his earthly life, He would make one last attempt to offer Himself as Messiah and King of the people of Israel.

To be able to reach thousands of people, He could not have chosen a better time to go to Jerusalem. Autumn's Festival of Tabernacles drew the greatest influx of pilgrims from within Israel and from the Mediterranean, Asia Minor and Europe. To finally entrap Him, the Pharisees were counting on His attendance at the Temple. Under the Sanhedrin's jurisdiction, they could move quickly with their plot to arrest Jesus.

Arriving halfway into the eight-day feast, He began teaching in the courts of the Temple.

"How did this man get such learning without having studied?" the people marveled. Yet the populace remained divided. "Some said, 'He is a good man.' Others replied, 'No, he deceives the people."

On the last day of the Festival of Tabernacles, an important ritual was enacted. The High Priest poured a golden pitcher of water down a silver tube at the side of the great altar. This act symbolically thanked God and reminded Him of their need for the rains He brought.

It was at the time of this hushed ceremony that Jesus cried "in a loud voice, 'If anyone is thirsty, let him come to me and drink. Whoever believes in me, as the Scripture has said, streams of living water will flow from within him.'"

Hearing these words, many Jewish people believed. But others feared spiritual and social ostracism by Temple officials and the Pharisees for being associated with Jesus.

It was at the Temple in Jerusalem that Jesus preached openly as to why God had sent Him.

New Testament Fulfillment

The Festival of Tabernacles was believed to be the Holy Day that anticipated the coming Kingdom of the Messiah. It was on the last day which was known as the "Great Day" of the festival that true believers anticipated the arrival of the Messiah. On that final day, Jesus suddenly cried out with what many understood was a claim of being the promised Messiah (John 7:37-41).

A Woman Caught In Adultery
JOHN 8:1-11

Old Testament Link

Ezekiel spoke against the leaders of Israel in his day, but also saw into the future. What he described condemned the coming leaders (shepherds) of His people (Ezekiel 34:4-5). So God spoke through the prophet, telling the children of Israel that one day He would come and be the Good Shepherd that they failed to be.

For hundreds of years, the scribes had been gatekeepers of the Law. Fearful that Israel would transgress God's commandments, they had interpreted the Mosaic Law into a myriad of detailed prohibitions, commandments and precepts.

No doubt their mission began as holy work; indeed, there were some among the Pharisees (particularly Nicodemus) who believed Jesus was the fulfillment of the Law. But by the time Jesus walked the earth, their many interpretations of the 613 Old Testament laws oppressed the people and blinded them from seeing God in their midst.

Some of the Pharisees thought they had found a way to trap Jesus into approving their license to reinterpret the Law. They had found Him teaching, perhaps amidst the marble floors of Solomon's porches, with an enrapt audience before Him. They dragged before Him a woman someone had caught in the act of adultery.

"In the Law, Moses commanded us to stone such women. Now what do you say?" the Pharisees asked. They hoped that Jesus would admit that the Mosaic Law was too harsh, thereby giving His tacit approval to their reinterpreting the Law.

His response to their question was totally unexpected: "If any of you is without sin, let him be the first to throw a stone at her." He had cleverly circumvented the Pharisee's trap, turning the issue from beyond the legal to the personal. One by one, each of these men walked away.

Addressing the woman, now without accusers, He said: "Neither do I condemn you." Far from condoning her behavior, He let her be free to change her ways. And, in His mercy, He forgave her transgression.

Just inside the walls of Jerusalem, the woman caught in adultery faced her accusers.

New Testament Fulfillment

The harsh treatment of the woman caught in adultery was one of many examples of how true devotion to God had been distorted. The Pharisees used this woman to try and trap Jesus. They didn't show concern for her; they were only concerned about their traditional interpretation of the Law. The Gospel of John contrasts these accusing shepherds with the "Good Shepherd of Israel." The Good Shepherd cared for both the sinful woman and the sinful Pharisee (John 10:11).

LAMENT FOR JERUSALEM
MATTHEW 23:37-39

Old Testament Link

God's love for Israel is like that of a mother for her child. The prophet Isaiah vividly describes his steadfast love: "Can a mother forget the baby at her breast and have no compassion on the child she has borne? Though she may forget, I will not forget you! See, I have engraved you on the palms of my hands; your walls are ever before me" (Isaiah 49:15-16).

The Pharisees warned Jesus: "Leave this place...Herod wants to kill you" (Luke 13:31). Their warning to Jesus still remains a mystery. It may have been motivated by compassion, or perhaps they hoped He would flee to Jerusalem, where He could be condemned under the Sanhedrin's authority. Jesus chose to reject their warning. No earthly despot could control the timetable His Father had appointed for His life and death.

In Jesus' message to Herod, the weight of the intrigues made Him cry out words that he would soon repeat on the Mount of Olives: "O Jerusalem, Jerusalem, you who kill the prophets and stone those sent to you, how often I have longed to gather your children together, as a hen gathers her chicks under her wings, but you were not willing!" (Luke 13:34).

The pouring forth of the Messiah's infinite compassion might have ended there. But the rejection of so great a love elicited one final, chilling prophecy: "Look, your house is left to you desolate. I tell you, you will not see me again until you say, 'Blessed is he who comes in the name of the Lord.'"

Soon after Jesus' ascension, in 70 A.D., the first part of His tragic prophecy was fulfilled. The Roman Emperor Titus completely destroyed Jerusalem, both the city of palaces and the Temple of cedarwood, marble and gold. The latter part of His prophecy has yet to come to pass. But Scripture tells us that it will: One day, the Lord will make Jerusalem "a heavy stone," a burdensome weight He will use to judge the nations of the earth.

The Lord promises: "On that day...I will make Jerusalem an unmoveable rock" (Zechariah 12:3).

Jerusalem was the capital city of God's chosen people, the ancestral home of King David, and the location of the Temple, the earthly dwelling place of God.

New Testament Fulfillment

Looking upon Jerusalem, Jesus wept over the sin of all men, for the Jew and also the Gentile (Romans 1:16). God's faithfulness to unfaithful Israel is a continual source of comfort and encouragement to genuine followers of Jesus.

The Resurrection of Lazarus
John 11:37-44

Old Testament Link

The idea of a physical resurrection was a well-established hope for Israel. Job first spoke of this hope: "I know that my Redeemer lives, and that in the end he will stand upon the earth. And after my skin has been destroyed, yet in my flesh I will see God" (Job 19:25-26). Daniel also prophesied of a resurrection: "Multitudes who sleep in the dust of the earth will awake: some to everlasting life, others to shame and everlasting contempt" (Daniel 12:2).

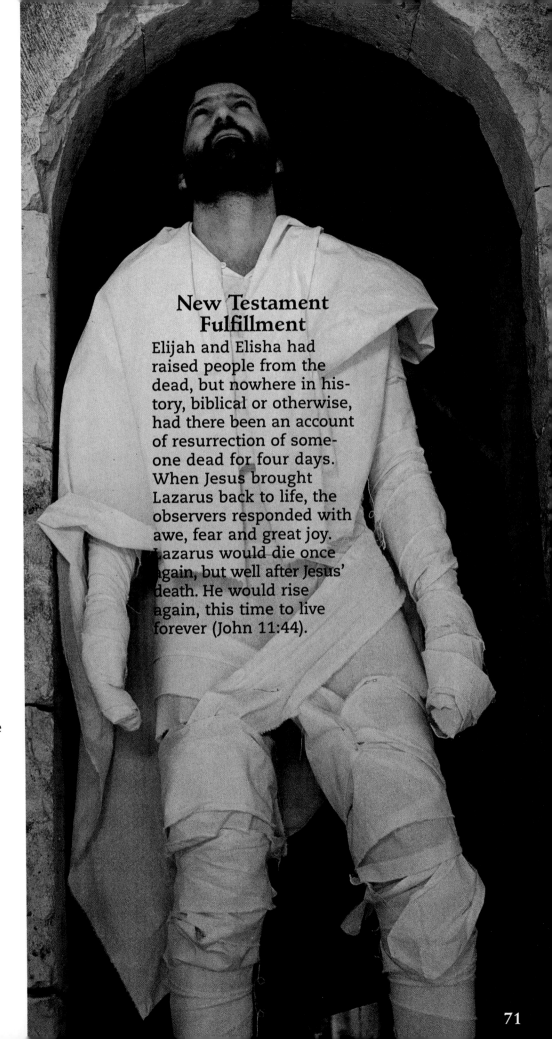

Lazarus and his sisters, Mary and Martha, were good friends of Jesus, and often while visiting the area He would stay overnight at their home in Bethany. Yet when informed of Lazarus' illness, Jesus delayed coming. Why?

Jesus told his disciples God would receive glory through Lazarus' illness, and He believed the miracle of resurrection would also strengthen the disciples' faith (John 11:14-15).

Arriving in Bethany, Jesus met Martha, who told Him of her brother's death. Gently, He guided her, the disciples, and two millennia of believers with the words of eternal life: "I am the resurrection and the life. He who believes in me will live, even though he dies; and whoever lives and believes in me will never die. Do you believe this?"

"Yes, Lord," she told Him. "I believe you are the Christ, the Son of God, who was to come into the world."

Martha showed a peerless confession of faith. Later, when Martha and Mary offered to show Jesus where their brother lay, Jesus wept, and the crowd was moved by His love for Lazarus.

When Jesus asked that the stone covering Lazarus' tomb be moved, Martha balked: "But Lord, by this time there is a bad odor, for he has been there four days." She soon complied, however, and Jesus then prayed out loud, as a witness to God's power. Finally, facing the open tomb, Jesus cried: "Lazarus, come out!" And the man who had been dead walked into the light.

This miracle caused many in Jerusalem to believe in Him. The resurrection of Lazarus probably strengthened the faith of the disciples, but it did not win Jesus any favor with the religious leaders. In an ironic prophecy of His mission, the High Priest, Caiaphas, foretold Jesus' death, declaring to his colleague: "It is better for you that one man die for the people than that the whole nation perish."

Lazarus, resurrected from death by Jesus, emerged from his tomb.

New Testament Fulfillment

Elijah and Elisha had raised people from the dead, but nowhere in history, biblical or otherwise, had there been an account of resurrection of someone dead for four days. When Jesus brought Lazarus back to life, the observers responded with awe, fear and great joy. Lazarus would die once again, but well after Jesus' death. He would rise again, this time to live forever (John 11:44).

TRIUMPHANT ENTRY INTO JERUSALEM
MATTHEW 21:1-11

Old Testament Link

On the very first Passover, God instructed the Israelites to set aside a lamb on the tenth of the month (Exodus 12:2). On the fourteenth of the month they were to kill that lamb and apply the blood to their doorposts. The blood of that lamb would be a "sign" for the Angel of Death to "pass over" that house. Where there was blood there would be life.

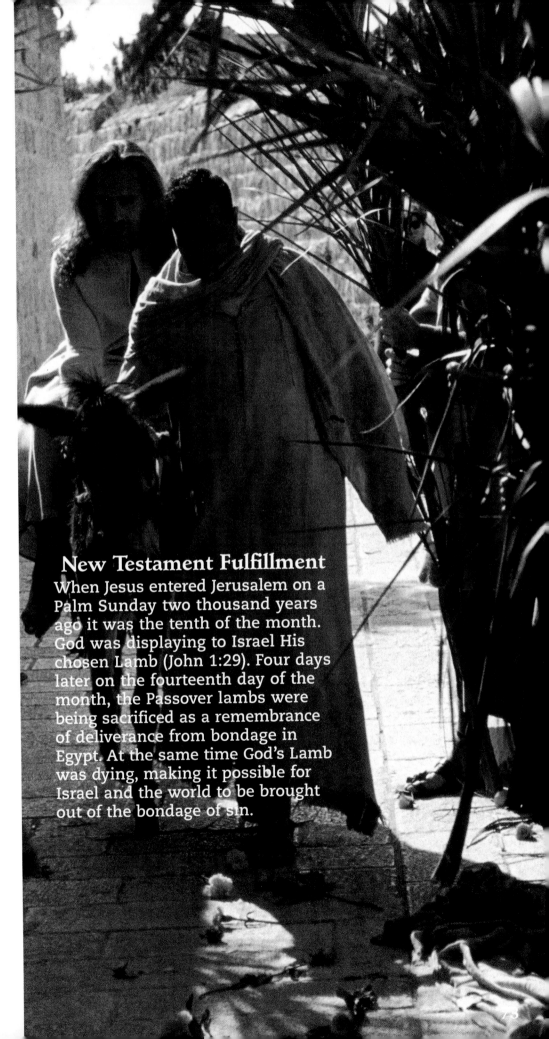

Just as the baptism of Jesus identified Him as Messiah, and the Transfiguration glorified Him, the Triumphant Entry presented Jesus to Israel as their Messiah and King. Yet, in what would prove to be the last week of His life, few knew of the extraordinary events that would soon take place.

In the very week of Jesus' appearance, Israelites from all over were also in Jerusalem to celebrate the Feast of Passover. It is ironic that while thousands of Jewish pilgrims searched the bazaars for a lamb to sacrifice for their family, the true Lamb of God was there to present Himself as the final atonement for their sins.

In perfect fulfillment of Messianic prophecy, Jesus entered Jerusalem on a young colt, a donkey as yet unridden. "See, your king comes to you, righteous and having salvation, gentle and riding on a donkey, on a colt, the foal of a donkey" (Zechariah 9:9).

As the adoring crowds spread palm branches before the donkey's path, they undoubtedly understood the Messianic implications. But if their expectations included a Messiah who would overturn their Roman oppressors, they were sadly mistaken.

Jesus, atop the donkey, wove His way down the steep and rugged Mount of Olives into the Kidron Valley. Jerusalem gradually came into view. At the sight of the city "he wept over it and said, 'If you, even you, had only known on this day what would bring you peace...'" (Luke 19:42). Precisely 445 years earlier on that day, the prophet Daniel had predicted the Messiah would enter Jerusalem (Daniel 9:25).

But Jerusalem's residents were unaware; the amazing events of that day became "hidden from your [Israel's] eyes" (Luke 19:42). The prophecy was fulfilled as Jesus rode through the gates of Jerusalem.

Walking from Jerico, Jesus sent the disciples ahead to the village of Bethphage, on the slope of the Mount of Olives. The disciples brought back a donkey for Jesus to ride.

New Testament Fulfillment

When Jesus entered Jerusalem on a Palm Sunday two thousand years ago it was the tenth of the month. God was displaying to Israel His chosen Lamb (John 1:29). Four days later on the fourteenth day of the month, the Passover lambs were being sacrificed as a remembrance of deliverance from bondage in Egypt. At the same time God's Lamb was dying, making it possible for Israel and the world to be brought out of the bondage of sin.

Old Testament Link

The prophet Isaiah saw a day when the Gentiles (nations) would come and offer praise, prayer, and sacrifices on God's holy mountain in Jerusalem. "…For my house will be called a house of prayer for all nations" (Isaiah 56:7).

Gazing up at the gates of Jerusalem only moments earlier, Jesus had wept over the city. The scene soon darkened by Divine decree. The coming events would fill the Chief Priests with fear and put them on a collision course with Jesus.

Entering the Temple courts, Jesus drove out those who sold the sacrificial animals and exchanged the foreign monies. The money-changers' practices began with good intentions, servicing the pilgrims who had traveled long distances. But soon the merchants and money-changers set up their booths in the Court of the Gentiles. The money-changers exchanged all secular currency for Temple currency — the only kind the merchants would accept. This desecration was at the heart of Jesus' "anger" when He declared: "Is it not written: 'My house will be called a house of prayer for all nations [Gentiles]? But you have made it a den of robbers" (Mark 11:17).

The pilgrims, who had often been victimized by the unscrupulous Temple merchants, rallied to Jesus' side. The Chief Priests could not dismiss the popular Jewish support Jesus had. Their fear was that the Jewish people would make Him king, in direct opposition to Caesar. The only way they could avoid the full wrath of Rome and save the Jewish people, they thought, was to eliminate Jesus. "Thus the High Priest Caiaphas declared: 'It is better

New Testament Fulfillment

The descendants of Israel had hardened their hearts towards the Gentiles. They hindered the Gentiles from worship and prohibited reconciliation to God through the sacrifices in the Temple. When Jesus cleansed the Temple of greedy merchants, His actions indicated that the time was near when Gentiles would be called "sons of the Living God" (Romans 9:26).

for you that one man die...than that the whole nation perish" (John 11:50).

Inside the Temple the children greeted Jesus with shouts of "Hosanna to the Son of David" — an unmistakable reference to the Messiah and his divine origin. At this, the Chief Priests cringed. "Do you hear what these children are saying?" they asked him.

"Yes," Jesus answered. "From the lips of children and infants [God has] ordained praise."

His explanation fell on deaf ears and hard hearts.

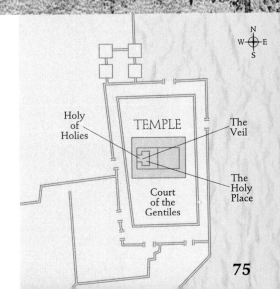

This is the second time Jesus cleared the Temple in the Court of the Gentiles. The first time was after the miracle at Cana.

A POOR WIDOW'S GIFT
LUKE 21:1-4

Old Testament Link

Isaiah was used by God to call Israel back to Himself. In the very first chapter of Isaiah, the prophet rebuked Israel for her gifts and offerings: "Stop bringing meaningless offerings!" (Isaiah 1:13). God wanted Israel's heart, not just meaningless offerings.

Jesus continued to amaze His followers as He taught in the Temple courts. However, the Chief Priests and some leaders continued to seek ways of publicly discrediting Him. One of their methods was to send earnest looking but deceptive listeners who posed troubling questions to the Master.

Jesus sharply pointed out the hypocrisy of these listeners and high-profile leaders. He accused them of parading their righteousness before men, desiring public recognition, and making a great show of their lengthy prayers.

To contrast this behavior, He directed the disciples' attention to a poor widow just steps away in the Court of the Women. The steady stream of worshippers often made a public show of their lavish tithing. Josephus the historian estimated that the Temple treasury regularly contained over $6 million in cash and precious vessels, by today's standards. The poor widow was probably ashamed of her meager contribution and most likely clutched the two copper coins in her hand so no one could see.

The denomination of the coins was so low that it was unlawful to tithe anything less — her gift was worth $\frac{1}{96}$ part of a denar, or the equivalent of ¼ of today's penny.

Jesus made sure the crowd understood that God was more pleased with this woman's offering than the lavish offerings of her more affluent brethren.

"I tell you the truth," He said, "this poor widow has put in more than all the others. All these people gave their gifts out of their wealth; but she out of her poverty put in all she had to live on." God's standard of measurement, Jesus implied, was not the size of the gift, but what was left in the giver's heart after it was offered.

Jesus was in the area of the Temple called the Court of the Women. The treasury was located nearby. There were seven boxes in which men could deposit their Temple tax and six boxes for freewill offerings like the one the poor widow gave.

New Testament Fulfillment

God called all followers to surrender not just a tenth of their wealth to Him (the standard tithe of Jesus' day), but rather their time, talent and treasure. Real worship, wrote the apostle Paul, is surrendering our whole lives to the Lord (Romans 12:1). The widow of Luke 21 demonstrated such total commitment by her gift to the Temple.

PREPARING THE PASSOVER MEAL
MATTHEW 26:17-19

Old Testament Link

The Law required that the person offering a sacrifice personally kill the animal after laying his hands on it (Leviticus 1:4-5). The blood of the animal would then be offered by the priests on the altar on the person's behalf. The blood represented the life of the animal and it was offered as a substitute for the sins of the offerer. Thus God was punishing sin by accepting a replacement for the sinner (Lev. 17:11).

The Passover was one night and one meal, but the Feast of Unleavened Bread, which was celebrated with it, continued for a week. Every spring in His life, Jesus had eaten the Passover meal with His family. This feast of freedom joyfully commemorated the night the Angel of Death passed over all the Jewish people who placed the blood of the lamb across their doorposts. The first born of the Egyptians and those who did not follow God's command were slain.

Jesus desired to share His last Passover meal with His disciples.

He entrusted Peter and John with the considerable preparations for the meal. First, they had to enter Jerusalem and search the many bazaars and merchants to purchase a spotless lamb. The lamb had to be an unblemished one year-old male. Then they had to bring it before the priests to be examined. Their sacrifice approved, they were then to wait in line at the Temple court with the animal.

The wait could be interminable. The historian Josephus estimated that 256,000 lambs were sacrificed on that Passover.

When their turn came, Peter and John were to cut the throat of the lamb and drain out the blood. Catching the blood in gold and silver bowls, the Temple Priests surrounding the Great Altar then turned and poured the blood on the altar. Then the lamb was skinned, and the fat and certain

New Testament Fulfillment

When Peter and John went to offer the lamb for the last Passover supper of Jesus, they did not understand that He would be their sacrifice. John the Baptist called Jesus "the Lamb of God" (John 1:29). He would take the punishment upon Himself and provide for atonement and reconciliation to God (1 Peter 2:24).

...rgans were reserved for sacrifice ...n the Great Altar.

With strains of the Levitical ...riests' Hallel (Psalm 118 sung as a ...ymn during the Passover sacrifice) ...till ringing in their ears, Peter and ...ohn rushed to the upper room Jesus ...ad designated. By Law, the lamb ...ad to be roasted before sunset. Still, ...heir work was not complete. There ...as unleavened bread (matzoh) to ...repare, wine to purchase and spe- ...ial foods to prepare.

As evening fell, Peter and John rested from their work. For the Master and His disciples, it would be their last supper together.

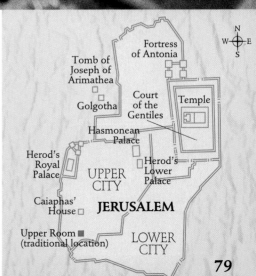

Near King David's tomb in Jerusalem, the disciples met a man carrying a pitcher of water. He led them to an upper room.

WASHING THE DISCIPLES' FEET
JOHN 13:3-11

Old Testament Link

Under the Law, if a man became indebted to a fellow Israelite and couldn't repay, he would be enslaved. He would remain in that condition until the debt was paid or the seventh year had passed, when he would be released. However, he could choose to remain a servant because of his love for his master, becoming a bondslave (Deuteronomy 15:12-17).

During their time in the upper room celebrating the Passover, the disciples began to argue about who was the greatest among them. Jesus quickly pointed out that such self-seeking was the way Gentiles, not Jews, behaved. "The kings of the Gentiles lord it over them...but you are not to be like that" (Luke 22:25-26).

Later, no doubt remembering the incident, Jesus showed how servants should act as He washed the disciples' feet. In stunned silence the 12 watched as Jesus removed his robe and girded Himself with a towel. This was a gesture connected with the lowliest servants. When He came to Peter, he resisted.

"No," said Peter, "you shall never wash my feet."

"Unless I wash you, you have no part with me."

"Then, Lord," Simon Peter replied, "not just my feet but my hands and my head as well!"

"A person who has had a bath needs only to wash his feet; his whole body is clean." Jesus made deft reference to one of the common practices of the day. Bathing was done at public baths. However, after just a short walk from the baths, one's feet became soiled with dust and dirt. Consequently, a basin was kept in most homes just to wash one's feet upon entering.

By virtue of Jesus' divinity, it would have been more appropriate

New Testament Fulfillment

In Romans 1:1, Paul describes himself as a servant of Jesus Christ. Paul saw himself as a bond-slave, one who freely chose to be a servant of his master. A true follower of Christ will be first a servant of God and then, like Jesus, a servant of man.

or the disciples to serve Him. ut the disciples probably did not nderstand the significance of what e had done. Years later the apostle aul explained the importance of esus' startling action: "Who, being n the very nature God, did not con-ider equality with God something o be grasped, but made himself othing, taking the very nature of servant..." (Philippians 2:6-7).

By washing the disciples' feet, esus demonstrated that His follow-ers were to move into the world serving God, serving each other and serving all people to whom they took the message of salvation.

Celebrating His last Passover in the upper room in Jerusalem, Jesus knew He would not leave the city alive.

81

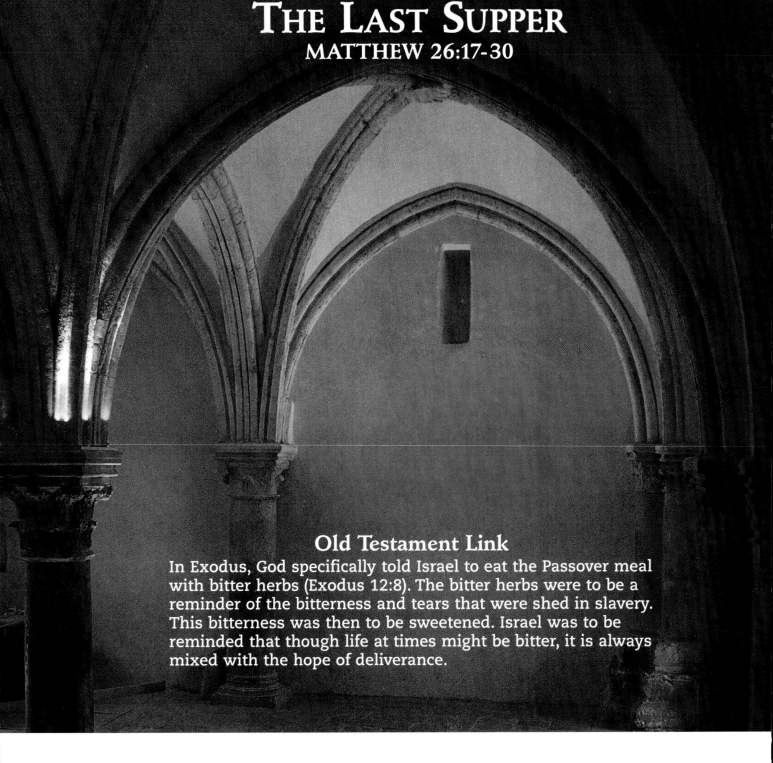

THE LAST SUPPER
MATTHEW 26:17-30

Old Testament Link
In Exodus, God specifically told Israel to eat the Passover meal with bitter herbs (Exodus 12:8). The bitter herbs were to be a reminder of the bitterness and tears that were shed in slavery. This bitterness was then to be sweetened. Israel was to be reminded that though life at times might be bitter, it is always mixed with the hope of deliverance.

Jesus must have smiled warmly at Peter and John as He entered the upper room. He did not regret entrusting them with the important details of preparing the Passover. The table was set with all the symbolic elements of the 1500 year-old freedom feast: the platter of unleavened bread (matzoh) to commemorate the Jewish Exodus from Egypt, when in their haste to leave there was no time to let their bread rise; the bitter herbs, which recalled the bitter-ness of the Israelites' enslavement by Pharaoh; the wine and finally the charoseth, a sweet paste of apples, wine and cinnamon, the color of brick, remembering the mortar Israel used to build the pyramids. Finally, of course, there was the Passover lamb.

As a feast of freedom, the Passover meal was a happy occasion. The participants traditionally reclined around the table, luxuriating in their status as free men.

Jesus and the disciples reclined, until He could hold back no more.

"And while they were eating, he said, 'I tell you the truth, one of you will betray me." His confession shocked those at the table. Stricken each one asked: "Surely not I, Lord?"

Peter leaned back to the disciple next to Jesus (probably John) and, his voice a whisper, asked the disciple to ask Jesus who the betrayer was.

"It is the one to whom I will give this piece of bread," Jesus answered

New Testament Fulfillment

In John 13 the Lord gave Judas the bitter herbs. Instead of reminding him of the bitterness of his forefathers in Egypt, his thoughts focused on the bitterness of Jesus' failure to bring Israel to greatness and glory. He left with the taste of bitterness in his mouth (John 13:21-30). The rest of the disciples partook of the charoseth and were reminded of the hope of God's redemption.

(John 13:26). The "bread" was an important part of the Passover meal. On a piece of unleavened bread, Jesus placed pieces of the various Passover foods including the bitter herbs.

Eating the bitter herbs brought tears to the eyes and served as a vivid reminder of their forefathers tears in slavery. To His left, the place of highest honor, sat Judas.

"As soon as Judas took the bread, Satan entered into him" (John 13:27).

Leaving the table, with bitterness in his mouth, Judas bolted from the room. "He went out," the Scripture closes abruptly. "And it was night" (John 13:30).

After Judas left the Last Supper, he most likely went to Caiaphas' house nearby, where he met with the Chief Priests.

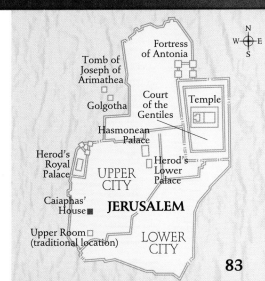

WORDS OF COMFORT DURING A LAST SUPPER
JOHN 14:1-4, 16-19

Old Testament Link

The Holy Spirit of God manifested Himself in many ways in the Old Testament, but the most pronounced was as fire. When God entered into His covenant to give the sons of Abraham the land of Canaan, it was in the form of a fiery torch (Genesis 15:17). When God gave His covenant of the Law on Mt. Sinai, He appeared again in the form of fire (Exodus 19:18), and when He led them through the wilderness it was in the form of a pillar of fire by night (Exodus 14:21).

During His final Passover meal, the Last Supper, Jesus had been trying to tell the disciples what they would not, or could not, hear. He was telling them good-bye.

"My children, I will be with you only a little while longer...Where I am going, you cannot come" (John 13:33).

In their minds, perhaps the disciples thought that Jesus would soon usher in the Messianic Kingdom. Hadn't He just told them at the table: "You are those who have stood by me in my trials. And I confer on you a kingdom...so that you may eat and drink at my table...and sit on thrones, judging the twelve tribes of Israel" (Luke 22:28-30). Of course, they were gravely mistaken if they thought Jesus was at this time going to usher in the Kingdom. The disciples still did not understand that before the Messiah entered into His glory, He first had to endure the suffering of the cross.

From the time He told them that He would be betrayed, a sad undertow began to pull them down. There was little that could be said to restore their hope. But He tried. He offered what should have been good news. He would send the Holy Spirit to comfort them.

"And I will ask the Father, and he will give you another Counselor to be with you forever — the Spirit of Truth." He promised not to leave them as orphans: "I will come to you."

New Testament Fulfillment

Jesus said: "The Counselor, the Holy Spirit, whom the Father will send in my name, will teach you all things and will remind you of everything I have said to you" (John 14:26). When this promise was fulfilled, the Holy Spirit came in the form of fire (Acts 2:3-4). As the pillar of fire had led the Israelites through the wilderness, the disciples of Jesus were led through the wilderness of life with the illuminating presence of God's Holy Spirit.

Earlier, in His most direct words of comfort, He assured them: "Do not let your hearts be troubled. Trust in God; trust also in me. In my Father's house are many rooms; if it were not so, I would have told you. I am going there to prepare a place for you. And if I go and prepare a place for you, I will come back and take you to be with me that you also may be where I am." There are few verses in Scripture that describe eternal life, but they are rich with promises.

Having comforted them, He drew to a close the most intimate fellowship He had known on earth. "I will not speak with you much longer, for the prince of this world is coming...Come now; let us leave" (John 14:30-31).

In the Essene community, where the upper room was located, Jesus comforted His disciples.

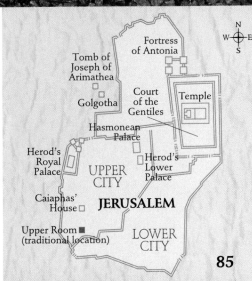

85

LESSONS FROM A VINEYARD
JOHN 15:1-16

Old Testament Link

In the Old Testament the vine is used as an illustration of the Nation of Israel. Isaiah complained that Israel was producing sour grapes. Jeremiah rebuked the Israelites as a vine that had become wild and unmanageable (Psalm 80:8; Isaiah 5:1-7; Jeremiah 2:21).

His last night on earth, Jesus had precious little time and still much to teach His disciples. As they left the upper room and the Passover Supper, it was already evening. Within hours He would be arrested in Gethsemane, brought before Pilate and ultimately crucified. During His time of suffering and separation from the disciples, He would be unable to minister to them.

Passing a vineyard, He drew the disciples aside to reveal the secret of fulfilling His mission. He likened their relationship with Him and the Father as one like the relationship of the branches, vine and vinedresser.

Apart from their drawing sustenance from the vine, they could not be fruitful. "I am the vine; you are the branches. If a man remains in me and I in him, he will bear much fruit" (John 15:5). "My Father is the gardener," Jesus explained. "He cuts off every branch in me that bears no fruit, while every branch that does bear fruit he prunes so that it will be even more fruitful."

Interestingly, the Greek word for "cuts off" is traditionally translated as "lifts up." This usage reflects on the cultivation of vineyards in the Middle East, or any dry climate. To preserve moisture, the vines were permitted to hug the ground. But as soon as blossoms appeared, the vines were raised off the ground on sticks and rocks to allow the blossoms to germinate.

Branches that bore no fruit withered and were "picked up, thrown into the fire and burned." In Jesus' day the dry branches were used to heat ovens that baked bread. Once their usefulness as was exhausted they were only ashes and dust underfoot.

From this practice the Messiah alluded to the Father placing branches (believers) where they had the best opportunity to be fruitful.

Jesus and those who followed were en route to Gethsemane when He taught about the vine and the branches.

New Testament Fulfillment

John 15 illustrates the Lord's continued desire for His people to produce fruit. The vinedresser's purpose is not to judge but to cultivate fruit. His purpose in cutting and pruning is to aid the faltering vine. Christ's followers must be attached to Him (the vine) in order to produce fruit. To be without fruit means that the Lord's goal for a life has been frustrated.

THE AGONY OF GETHSEMANE
MATTHEW 26:36-46

Old Testament Link

The separation that Jesus feared was necessary if He was to be our sin bearer. Every year on the Day of Atonement, the sins of the nation were placed on the scapegoat named "Azazel" (literally, goat of removal; Leviticus 16:10). This goat carried the sins of the nation into the wilderness, where it eventually died (Leveticus 16:21-22). The prophet Isaiah foretold the Messiah would also carry away our sins with His death (Isaiah 53:6).

There is no more graphic depiction of the Messiah's agony than of the tortured and gnarled trunks of the olive trees in Gethsemane. It was here that He spent His last hours before being betrayed and condemned to die.

Leaving the disciples with the admonition to "watch and pray," He walked further into the garden. Sensing all that lay before Him in the following days, He fell to the ground and prayed: "My Father, if it is possible, may this cup be taken from me."

The cup Jesus referred to probably was the bitter taste of separation from God — a necessary consequence of being made sin for us. God placed on Jesus the sins of all humanity and then had to hide His face from His beloved Son. For the sinless one, Jesus, who had never known a moment's separation from His Father, the anguish was so intense that He cried out. Jesus also may have thought that as a ransom for humanity, He might be consigned by a righteous God to some outer darkness. This fear of not being immediately redeemed from death may have been the cup He so feared to drink from.

His anguish was deep; physically He was in distress. Luke records that Jesus began to perspire profusely as He prayed: "and His sweat was like drops of blood falling to the ground" (Luke 22:44).

New Testament Fulfillment

In order for us to be made righteous, Jesus took our sins on Himself (2 Corinthians 5:21). This exchange took place as the prophets foretold when He "died on the tree," taking the curse that was due to us upon Himself (Galatians 3:13).

The Son of God was all alone during this dark hour. His three closest disciples had come with Him, yet they fell asleep. In spite of Jesus' request that they stay awake and pray, He found them slumbering three different times. His loneliness was both spiritual and physical.

Weeks later, only yards from that site, He would ascend to His Father from the Mount of Olives. But first there was the agony: the full cup of God's judgment for mankind's sin would have to be drained.

In the quiet of Gethsemane, away from the noise of Jerusalem, was where Jesus pondered His death for the sins of the world.

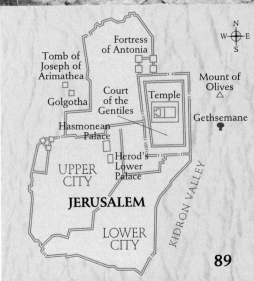

BETRAYED IN GETHSEMANE
MATTHEW 26:47-56

Old Testament Link

The rabbis recognized that Joseph, the beloved son of Jacob, was a foreshadow of the Messiah. Their recognition is due in part to his being sold as a slave. The prophet Zechariah was given a vision of Israel's rejection of her promised Messiah: she would give up the Messiah sent to her for the price of a slave, 30 pieces of silver (Exodus 21:32). In both cases the betrayals can be summed up with the words of Joseph: "God intended it for good, to accomplish...the saving of many lives" (Genesis 50:20).

Without Judas, the High Priests could not have found Jesus to arrest Him. But the traitor led the guards through the night with lanterns blazing to Gethsemane.

Gethsemane is the Greek form of the Hebrew word for "olive press." Probably the heart of this grove contained a press for the extracting of olive oil from the trees of the surrounding orchard. Gethsemane was a familiar place to Judas, who had often stayed there with the other disciples and Jesus. But this night it may have been harder to find, as Jerusalem was teeming with pilgrims visiting to celebrate the Passover. The valley between the Temple and the Mount of Olives was encamped with Temple-goers. Eventually, Judas sorted through the many campfires and led the Roman guards to the grove located at the foot of the mountain.

The Greek word *Kataphileo*, used to describe Judas' kiss, connotes something more than a peck on the cheek; it conveys great warmth and affection. Apparently, Judas made a great show of his supposed devotion. In contrast, Jesus' greeting was all the more chilling and minimal: "Friend, do what you came for."

As the soldiers arrested Him, Peter stepped up to defend the Lord. Once more Peter acted without really understanding the mission of the Messiah by wielding a sword. Peter failed to comprehend that Jesus came

New Testament Fulfillment

Judas received 30 pieces of silver to betray Jesus (Matthew 26:14-15), thus fulfilling Zechariah's prophecy.

o bring a heavenly, not a worldly kingdom. Jesus told Peter that He only ad to ask the Father, and legions f angels would be sent to His defense.

It would not be until after the esurrection and Peter's subsequent illing with God's Spirit, that he vould understand that the weapons f spiritual battle were not like hose of the world (1 Corinthians 0:4). In the account in John's Gospel, Jesus asks Peter: "Shall I not drink the cup, the Father has given

me?" In complete submission, Jesus followed the Father's plan, even unto death.

Outside the city walls and below the Mount of Olives, Judas led the Temple guards to Gethsemane.

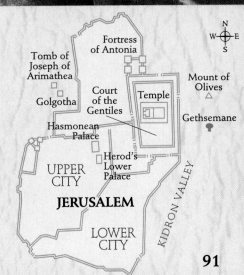

A DIVINE DECLARATION
MATTHEW 26:57-68

Old Testament Link
In Daniel 7:13-14 the Son of Man is described in terms of deity. This unique person would be "given authority, glory and sovereign power" over "all peoples, nations and men of every language" who would worship Him.

For Annas, High Priest Emeritus and father-in-law of Caiaphas, the arrest of Jesus was sweet revenge. Wasn't it the rabble-rousing Jesus who had cleansed the Temple, overturning the merchant's tables that were sanctioned by him?

At Caiaphas' house, Annas began questioning Him about His disciples and His message. Perhaps he was trying to determine how strong His following was in Jerusalem.

"I have spoken openly to the world," Jesus replied. When Annas had completed the interrogation (John 18:20-24), he sent Jesus back to Caiaphas.

The hearing before Caiaphas was a notable injustice. First, this night-time gathering of the Sanhedrin was illegal. Second, the witnesses were never ceremonially put under oath. But the greatest miscarriage of justice was the continued goading by Caiaphas to make Jesus testify

against Himself. Finally, two witnesses came forward, recounting Jesus' prophecy that He would destroy the Temple and rebuild it in three days (John 2:19).

At last Caiaphas had a charge that would stick. "Are you not going to answer?" But Jesus remained silent. Frustrated, Caiaphas cut to the heart of the matter: "I charge you under oath by the living God: Tell us if you are the Christ, the Son of God."

New Testament Fulfillment

When the High Priest Caiaphas placed Him under sacred oath, Jesus was bound by law to re-spond. His reply affirmed that He was the Messiah, and that He was the One spoken of in Daniel 7 (Matthew 26:63-64). The High Priest understood that Jesus was claiming to be God and so declared Him a blasphemer.

"Yes, it is as you say," Jesus replied, breaking His majestic silence. But I say to all of you: In the future you will see the Son of Man sitting at the right hand of the Mighty One and coming on the clouds of heaven."

Caiaphas and the Sanhedrin may not have understood the Messiah to also be divine. But in His confession, Jesus purposefully employed the references understood to be describing God and the Son of Man.

They had heard all they needed to hear. The charge of blasphemy stood. But Jesus had answered with a divine declaration: He was the Christ, the Son of God.

Annas sent Jesus to Caiaphas' home, not far from the upper room, to be questioned at night instead of in the Temple during the day.

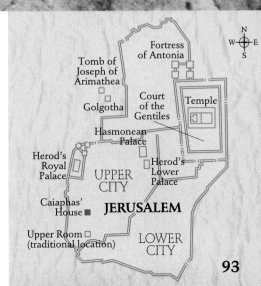

JERUSALEM

Fortress of Antonia · Tomb of Joseph of Arimathea · Court of the Gentiles · Temple · Golgotha · Hasmonean Palace · Herod's Royal Palace · Herod's Lower Palace · UPPER CITY · Caiaphas' House · Upper Room (traditional location) · LOWER CITY

PETER'S THREE DENIALS OF JESUS

MARK 14:66-72

Old Testament Link

In Zechariah 13:7 the prophet saw the followers of a shepherd fleeing in fear: "Strike the shepherd, and the sheep will be scattered." Ezekiel prophesied that God in the person of the Messiah would be the Shepherd who would seek His sheep.

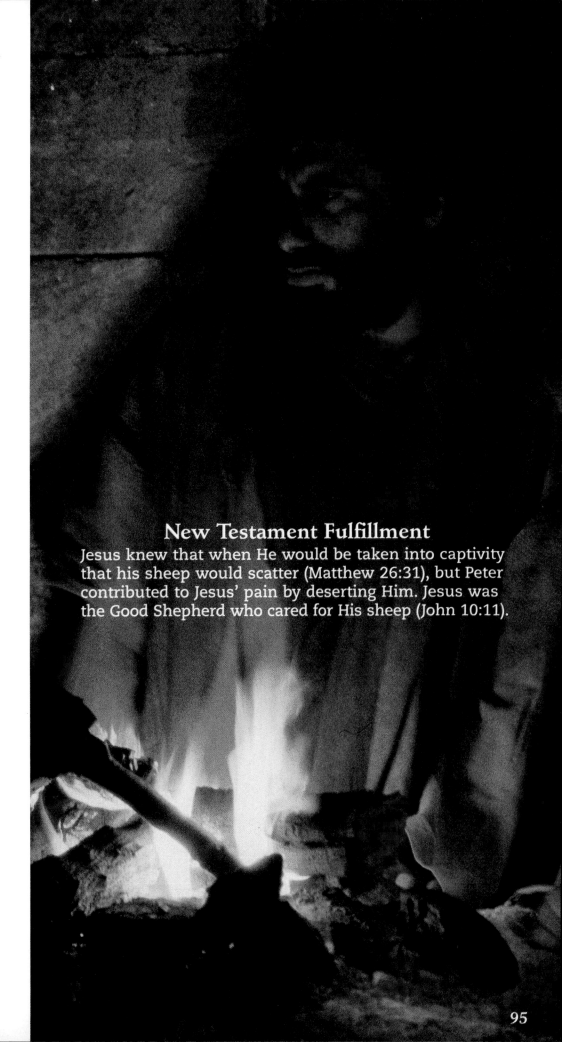

Hours earlier at the Last Supper, Peter pledged to follow the Lord even to death. Yet he would not follow Him into the house of the High Priest, waiting instead outside in the courtyard. Peter was the only one to follow Jesus that night, even if only at a distance.

As he warmed himself by a fire in the courtyard, Peter forgot Jesus' warning during their final supper together: "Simon, Simon, Satan has asked to sift you like wheat...I tell you Peter, before the rooster crows today, you will deny three times that you know me" (Luke 22:31-34).

He loved the Lord, but Peter felt both anger and fear.

Just then, from inside the house, the High Priest's voice split the night. "He has spoken blasphemy!" The High Priest's attendants would take this verdict as a license to severely beat Jesus, cruelly mocking Him.

Meanwhile, Peter stayed in the courtyard hoping to gather his courage and say something...anything! A servant woman peered closely at his face. "You were with Jesus of Galilee," she said.

An eternity passed, and finally Peter spoke. "Woman," he heard himself say, "I don't know the man." A wave of shame engulfed him.

Again, the woman asked him, and again he denied. As he feigned anger by calling down curses upon himself if he was lying, he denied Him a third time.

In the distance a cock crowed.

As Peter moved woodenly away from the fire to the gate, a rush of tears fogged his sight. Stumbling into the night, he remembered, understood and realized that the Lord knew him better than he knew himself.

The steps near Caiaphas' house are all that remain of his huge palace. John probably knew some of the servants at Caiaphas' house and was let in the courtyard with Peter.

New Testament Fulfillment

Jesus knew that when He would be taken into captivity that his sheep would scatter (Matthew 26:31), but Peter contributed to Jesus' pain by deserting Him. Jesus was the Good Shepherd who cared for His sheep (John 10:11).

On Trial Before Pilate
JOHN 18:28-38

Old Testament Link

King David spoke prophetically of the events that would take place when he wrote: "The kings of the earth take their stand and the rulers gather together against the Lord and against His Anointed One" (Psalm 2:2).

Once Jesus made a divine declaration that He was "the Christ, the Son of God," the High Priest charged Him with blasphemy. After hearing His claim and the charge of blasphemy, the Sanhedrin, the ruling religious body consisting of 71 elders and scribes, condemned Him to death.

As subjects of Rome, the religious leaders did not have the authority to carry out an execution. As dawn was breaking the leaders left Caiaphas' home and went to the Fortress Antonio, taking Jesus with them, hoping to enlist the support of the Roman procurator Pontius Pilate. This must have both amused and revulsed Pilate. Time after time he had clashed with his Jewish subjects, having little tolerance for their religious customs and sensitivities. Religion, superstition; it was all unimportant to Pilate. Standing on the building's porch he listened to the Sanhedrin's charges.

"Take him yourselves and judge him by your own law," said Pilate, once again revealing how tired he had grown of his Judean subjects. Realizing that they could not win support for condemning Jesus on religious grounds, the Sanhedrin sought to accuse Him of treason against Rome. "He opposes payment of taxes to Caesar and claims to be Christ, a king" (Luke 23:2).

With this new accusation, Pilate walked back into the praetorium

New Testament Fulfillment

In Acts 4:25-27, the Spirit of God revealed that the prophecy of King David was fulfilled when Jesus stood before Pilate and Herod.

here Jesus was being held. "Are you he king of the Jews?" Pilate asked.

"Yes, it is as you say," Jesus eplied.

Still Pilate saw no guilt in Jesus nd told this to the Chief Priests nd a crowd that had gathered. ilate's lack of support aroused a uror of protest. Fearing a riot by the rowd, and their threat to provoke he Emperor Tiberius in Rome, with hom Pilate had already lost favor, e relented. Trying to avoid further

trouble, Pilate dispatched Jesus to Herod, permitting him to determine His fate. The trial before Pilate probably took less than an hour.

Jesus was tried in Pilate's praetorium, which was near or in the Fortress Antonia.

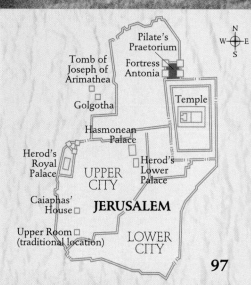

A Flogging And A Crown Of Thorns
JOHN 19:1-6

Old Testament Link
The prophet Isaiah foretold that the promised Messiah or "Servant" would be crushed for our iniquities. He further stated that the punishment that brought us peace was upon him, and by his wounds we are healed (Isaiah 53:5).

Jesus was the One on trial, but Pilate also was being judged. Pilate tried to remain disinterested and remote, but the motivations of his heart were being exposed. Inevitably, he would have to make a decision. Free Jesus as an innocent man or condemn Him to some form of punishment: beating, imprisonment, or death by crucifixion.

Pilate tried to shift the decision to Herod. If Herod found Him guilty, all the better; His blood would be on Herod's hands. But Herod sent Jesus back to Pilate, finding no guilt in Him.

Pilate decided to have Jesus flogged, thinking this would satisfy His accusers, and then release Him.

A Roman flogging was often harsh enough to be lethal. The instrument of punishment was similar to a "cat 'o nine" tails with pieces of bone and iron attached to the lashes. These objects would pull pieces of skin away from the victim's back and draw blood. A typical flogging consisted of 39 lashes. Isaiah had predicted that the Messiah would be beaten on the back and face, His beard would be plucked out and He would be mocked and spit upon. Jesus' flogging was so severe, He was unable to carry His cross.

When it was over, the Roman soldiers dressed Jesus in a purple robe and put a crown of thorns on His head. As the thorns pierced His forehead, a Roman soldier shouted in mock worship: "Hail, O king of the Jews!" and struck Him in the face. In His weakened condition, Pilate brought Jesus before the crowd: "Here is the man!" Pilate was hoping the crowd would see this pathetic form was no threat to them. But they would not relent.

"Crucify! Crucify!" they shouted.

Pilate answered: "You take him and crucify him. As for me, I find no basis for a charge against him."

Inside Antonia, a massive fortress with four impressive towers, Jesus was beaten and humiliated.

New Testament Fulfillment
The suffering of the Messiah made it possible for us to be reconciled to God. Peter taught that part of our reconciliation was made possible by the wounds that Jesus suffered (1 Peter 2:24).

MOCKING AND HUMILIATION
MARK 15:16-20

Old Testament Link

The prophet Isaiah gave a tragic picture of the mocking of a Messiah 700 years before Jesus was born: "He was oppressed and afflicted, yet he did not open his mouth; he was led like a lamb to the slaughter, and as a sheep before her shearers is silent, so he did not open his mouth" (Isaiah 53:7).

Five separate times, Pilate pointed to the innocence of Jesus. Still the mob called out for His crucifixion: "We have a law, and according to that law he must die, because he claimed to be the Son of God" (John 19:7). These words made Pilate shiver with fear.

As he sat on the judgment seat, Pilate received a message sent by his wife. "Don't have anything to do with that innocent man," the message read, "for I have suffered a great deal today in a dream because of him." Pilate returned to the inside of the praetorium with his wife's plea echoing in his mind.

The entire company of Roman soldiers was now taunting Jesus. As the detested occupiers of Jerusalem, these young soldiers seized the opportunity to lash out on Jesus the hatred they felt for their Jewish charges. As the crown of thorns dug into Jesus' brow, the purple robe hanging over His bloodied frame, they gave Him a reed scepter. "Hail, king of the Jews!" they proclaimed once more.

Again and again they struck Him and spit on him. Falling on their knees, they paid mock homage to Him.

Pilate called a momentary halt to the soldiers' cruel theatrics.

"Where do you come from?" he asked Jesus, but Jesus gave him no answer. "Do you refuse to speak to me?" Pilate asked. "Don't you realize I have power either to free you or to crucify you?"

"You would have no power over me if it were not given to you from above" (John 19:9-11).

Such invincible words from one so broken soon unnerved and moved the Roman governor. "From then on, Pilate tried to set Jesus free" (John 19:12).

Jesus was beaten and spit upon by Roman soldiers expressing their hatred for their Jewish charges.

New Testament Fulfillment

Following the verbal thrashing and repeated beatings of Jesus by the Roman soldiers, His silence amazed Pilate (John 19:9). Jesus refused to defend Himself knowing that God had given this cup of sorrows and death to drink (Luke 22:42).

WASHING HANDS OF INNOCENT BLOOD
MATTHEW 27:21-26

Old Testament Link

In Deuteronomy 21, the Law made a provision for a city to be forgiven of an unsolvable homicide. The neck of a heifer would be broken, and the priests would wash their hands over the dead animal. They would then declare: "Our hands did not shed this blood, nor did our eyes see it done" (Deuteronomy 21:7).

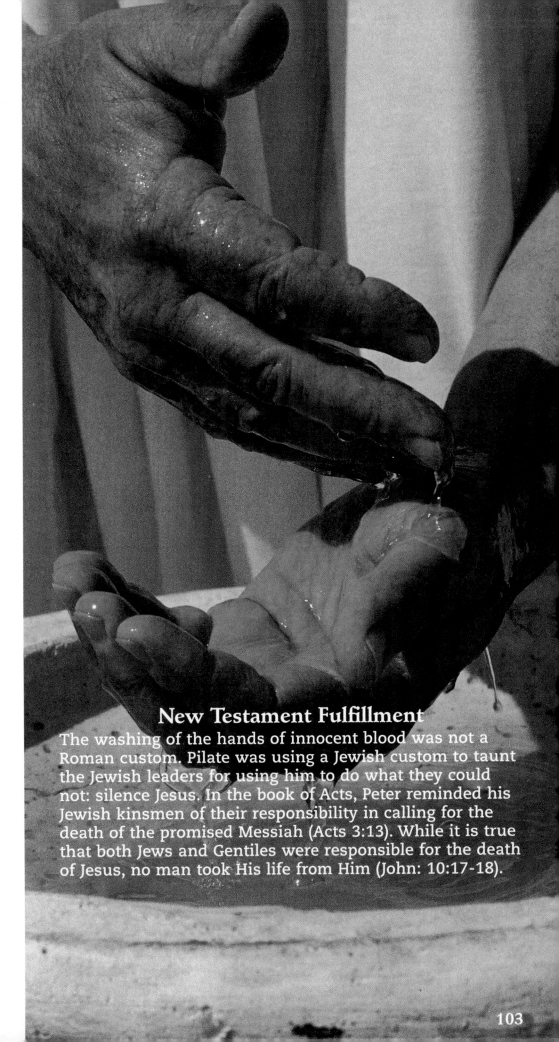

Convinced that Jesus should be freed, Pilate approached the crowd once again. But their shouts to crucify Jesus and free Barabbas, a criminal, were relentless. "Why? What crime has he committed?" asked Pilate (Mark 15:14).

How strange Pilate must have felt, a man who had turned a scornful eye on anything resembling religion or superstition, to suddenly be defending the King of the Jews. During the previous hour, he had parried arguments with Jesus. When the Master revealed that He had come into the world "to testify to the truth," Pilate had answered: "What is truth?" (John 18:38).

Pilate's good intentions, however, were short lived. The mob jolted him back to reality with a disturbing threat: "If you let this man [Jesus] go, you are no friend of Caesar. Anyone who claims to be a king opposes Caesar." Pilate had already earned a strong rebuke from Emperor Tiberius for his insensitive treatment of the Jews. Pilate could not afford another. To make matters worse, the emperor had been enraged by the treason of Pilate's trusted friend and functionary, Sejanus: the man who had urged his appointment as procurator! A charge of treason against Pilate could cost him everything — even his life.

When Pilate saw that he was getting nowhere with his desire to save Jesus, and had instead created an uproar, he washed his hands in front of the crowd. This practice was not new to him; ritual hand-washing was a widespread custom to symbolize innocence. "I am innocent of this man's blood," he said. Brazenly, the people shot back: "Let his blood be on us and on our children!"

On this very spot 30 years later, the Roman governor spilled the blood 3600 men by crucifixion against Jerusalem's walls.

It was here in the Fortress of Antonia that Pilate washed his hands of any responsibility.

New Testament Fulfillment
The washing of the hands of innocent blood was not a Roman custom. Pilate was using a Jewish custom to taunt the Jewish leaders for using him to do what they could not: silence Jesus. In the book of Acts, Peter reminded his Jewish kinsmen of their responsibility in calling for the death of the promised Messiah (Acts 3:13). While it is true that both Jews and Gentiles were responsible for the death of Jesus, no man took His life from Him (John: 10:17-18).

Carrying The Cross
Luke 23:26-31

V:
SIMONI-CYRENAEO
CRUX IMPONITUR.
ST:

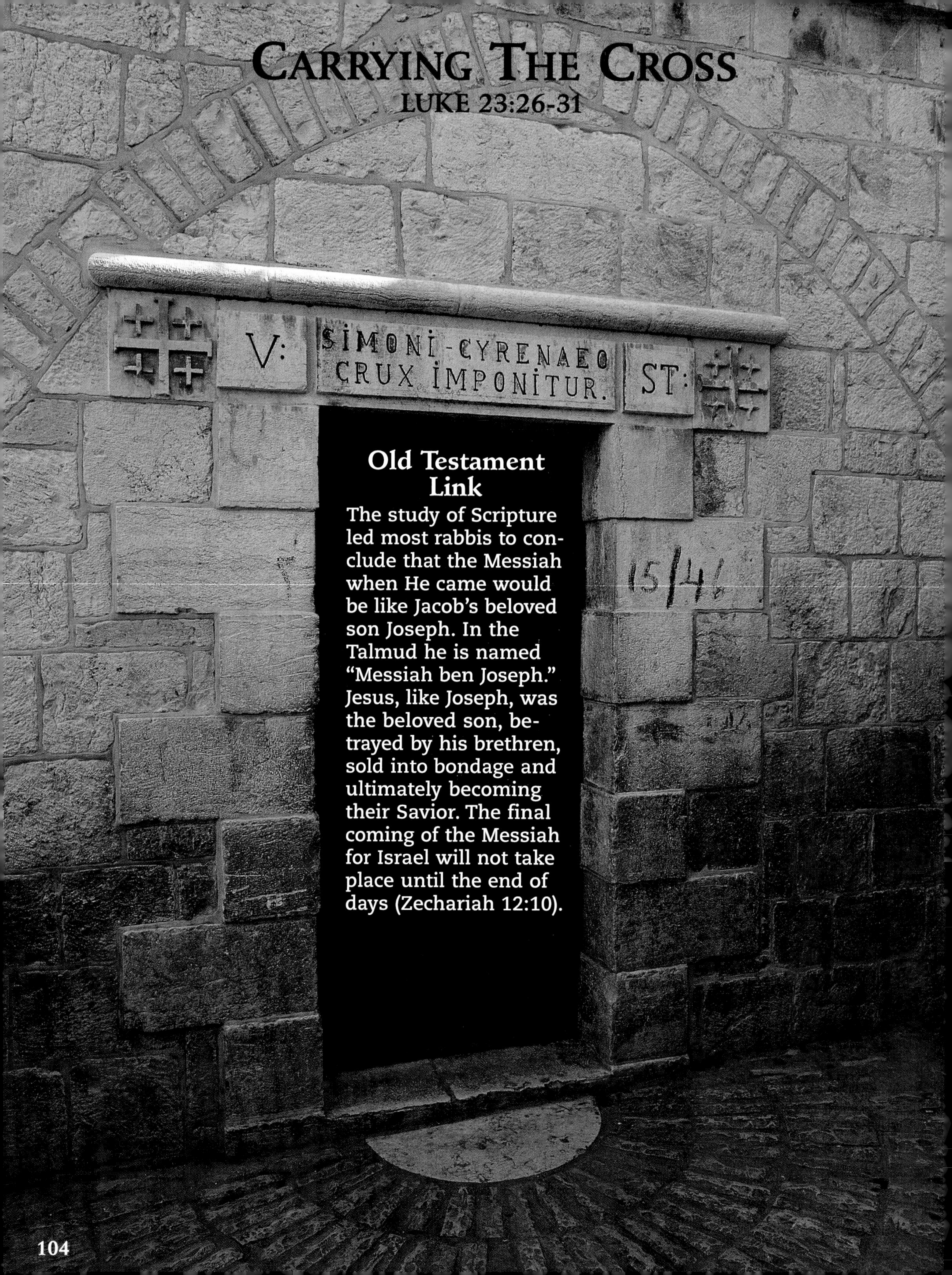

Old Testament Link

The study of Scripture led most rabbis to conclude that the Messiah when He came would be like Jacob's beloved son Joseph. In the Talmud he is named "Messiah ben Joseph." Jesus, like Joseph, was the beloved son, betrayed by his brethren, sold into bondage and ultimately becoming their Savior. The final coming of the Messiah for Israel will not take place until the end of days (Zechariah 12:10).

The violent flogging that Jesus endured made Him unable to carry His cross to the place of crucifixion. The broad crossbeam that the Roman soldiers hefted onto His shoulders pressed into His lacerated flesh and bowed Him to the ground. Seeing they would make no progress through the streets this way, the soldiers pressed a passerby into service to carry Jesus' cross.

Simon from Cyrene was on his way to Jerusalem to celebrate the Passover. Cyrene was a city in North Africa with a large Jewish population. Legend has it that Simon might have been a Jewish proselyte, but as a witness of the passion and crucifixion, he became an early follower of the Messiah.

The melancholy procession wove its way through the streets, and "A large number of people followed him, including women who mourned and wailed for him. Jesus turned and said to them, 'Daughters of Jerusalem, do not weep for me; weep for yourselves and for your children. For the time will come when you will say, "Blessed are the barren women, the wombs that never bore and the breasts that never nursed!" There was no sarcasm in His voice. In His omniscience, He saw the day when Jerusalem would fall under invading armies.

Josephus, the secular historian, witnessed the wrath of a Roman governor who, in around 70 A.D., actually exhausted the supply of wood as he crucified Jerusalem's citizenry along her walls. Jesus, himself a prophet, foresaw the coming persecution, including starvation and death, and felt compassion for the Jewish people — even as He staggered along the *Via Dolorosa* (the way of the cross) to Calvary and death.

As Jesus was led to be crucified through the streets of Jerusalem, He could no longer carry His cross, and Simon of Cyrene was given the burden.

New Testament Fulfillment

In the first gospel message of Peter, many people of Israel learned that the One who suffered and was crucified was the beloved of the Father. Hearing this "they were cut to the heart" and asked Peter what they could do. He told them they should repent and be baptized (Acts 2:36-38).

THE CRUCIFIXION
JOHN 19:17-24

Old Testament Link

The prophet Isaiah foretold the coming Messiah would be "...oppressed and afflicted, yet he did not open his mouth; he was led like a lamb to the slaughter, and as a sheep before her shearers is silent, so he did not open his mouth" (Isaiah 53:7). Jesus was God's perfect sacrificial lamb. He was born in a place where animals were kept, cradled in an animal feeding trough and viewed by lowly shepherds. All the signs of the Messiah by the Old Testament prophets would point to Jesus as the Lamb of God.

By the third hour, 9:00 a.m., Jesus was taken to a hilly rise outside of Jerusalem, called Golgotha. The soldier leading the procession displayed a small board listing the condemned's crime for all to see. Pilate had the board inscribed "King of the Jews," knowing this would inflame the Chief Priests and the Sanhedrin. Upon hearing that Pilate had mocked them, the Chief Priests left the Temple and the Passover ceremonies to demand that he change it. "What I have written, I have written," he answered.

Knowing the great pain Jesus was about to endure, the soldiers offered Him wine mixed with myrrh to deaden His consciousness (Matthew 27:34). He refused.

Even though Jewish people normally executed people by stoning, Isaiah predicted that the suffering Servant would be "pierced for our transgressions" (Isaiah 53:5).

Through His hands they drove iron nails into the beam. With ropes they hoisted Him to a post that was nailed to an olive tree, pruned for the occasion. To this post His feet were nailed. Not as high as portrayed in medieval paintings, for the soles of His feet were barely 24 inches from the ground.

Beneath Him, the soldiers divided His clothing. But when they came to His undergarment they paused. It was seamless, unlike most garments of the day which were many pieces sewn together. It could not be divided equally between them. Significantly, this was the same type of garment the High Priest wore. A woman who had benefited from His ministry probably made Him this noble garment.

"Let's not tear it," the soldiers said. Instead, they cast lots, fulfilling what was said thousands of years earlier. "[They] cast lots for my clothing" (Psalm 22:18).

This place called "The Skull," or Golgotha, was outside Jerusalem along a main road. Many executions took place there so the Romans could use them as examples.

New Testament Fulfillment
Paul explained why Jesus was crucified on a "tree." He taught that "Christ redeemed us from the curse of the law by becoming a curse for us, for it is written: 'Cursed is everyone who is hung on a tree" (Galatians 3:13).

MIRACULOUS SIGNS AT THE CRUCIFIXION
MATTHEW 27:38-54

Old Testament Link

God commanded that a curtain or a "veil" should separate the Holy Place from the Holy of Holies (Exodus 26:33). Only once a year, on the Day of Atonement, would the High Priest be allowed to enter the Holy of Holies. There, blood would be placed on the mercy seat, and God's covenant with Israel would be renewed (Leviticus 16, Numbers 29:7-11).

Just as supernatural phenomenon accompanied the birth of Jesus, His death would also be marked by miraculous signs. By the noon hour, He had already endured the insults hurled at Him by the thief on the cross next to Him and the taunts of onlookers: "He saved others; let him save himself" (Luke 23:35). Now, as if to obscure this shameful scene from public scrutiny, a heavy darkness covered the earth. This shadowy eclipse darkened all of Jerusalem.

For three hours this darkness shrouded the worst physical agonies that Jesus suffered. Then at three o'clock "Jesus cried out in a loud voice, 'Eloi, Eloi, lama sabachthani,'" meaning, "My God, my God, why have you forsaken me?" Mistakenly thinking Jesus was calling for the prophet Elijah, the bystanders offered Him wine vinegar.

Refusing, He "cried out again in a loud voice, [and] gave up His spirit." At that moment the curtain (veil) of the Temple was torn in two from top to bottom. Only a few yards away, thousands of young, unblemished lambs were being slaughtered on Israel's behalf.

Whether it was the earthquake itself a resultant disturbance, the huge curtain of the Temple split. This curtain, 60 feet tall by 30 feet wide, separated the Most Holy Place and the Holy of Holies from defilement. The Holy Place was open, by way of the Messiah's sacrifice, to all

New Testament Fulfillment

When Jesus died on the cross the veil was torn from top to bottom (Matthew 27:51). This was a sign to Israel that Jesus had entered the heavenly tabernacle to offer His blood (Hebrews 9).

The miraculous signs continued. The earth shook, rocks split, and as the earthquake continued. "The tombs broke open and the bodies of many holy people who had died were raised to life."

As the centurion and the soldiers witnessed the earthquake, they were terrified: "Surely he was the Son of God!" the centurion declared. He was watching the greatest miracle of all: the Son of God dying willingly for the sins of mankind.

Almost 1000 years before Jesus was crucified, the Spirit of God inspired David to write: "I am poured out like water, and all my bones are out of joint" (Psalm 22:14). David prophesied that the Messiah would suffer in this way.

Jesus was led to Golgotha, "The Skull," a hill outside of Jerusalem where executions were displayed for the people.

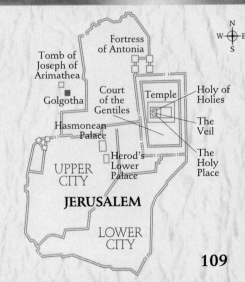

JERUSALEM

THE BURIAL OF JESUS
JOHN 19:31-42

Old Testament Link

The prophet Isaiah gave Israel more information about the details of the coming "Servant of the Lord" (Isaiah 53:9). "He was assigned a grave with the wicked, and with the rich in his death, though he had done no violence, nor was any deceit in his mouth."

Crucifixion was a slow, agonizing death that could last for days. Hanging from the hands, the body's weight bore down on the victim's lungs and made breathing difficult. A healthy man could take breaths as long as his legs could momentarily lift his body up for each breath.

The Pharisees sought to hasten the deaths of those at Golgotha. They wanted no bodies exposed to the elements, defiling the Passover Sabbath. And so, as the evening drew nigh and the soldiers observed that the thieves on either side of Jesus seemed to be using their legs to support their sagging bodies, the Romans broke their legs.

When they saw that Jesus was already dead, they pierced His side.

Joseph of Arimathea, an affluent member of the Sanhedrin and a secret follower of Jesus, asked Pilate's permission to claim the body. When Pilate consented, Joseph took the body down off the cross. He was accompanied by Nicodemus, another member of the Sanhedrin sympathetic to Jesus' ministry (John 3:1-15).

In a nearby garden, Joseph prepared the body for burial in a new tomb — his own — fulfilling Isaiah's prophecy that Jesus would receive a burial among the rich. Tearing the shroud into swatches, Joseph and Nicodemus wrapped the body with spices (aloe and myrrh) Nicodemus brought, and placed Jesus in the tomb.

Fearing Jesus' promise to rise from the dead (or to prevent the disciples from stealing the body), the Pharisees obtained guards from Pilate to stand watch. The Roman guards placed a seal on a large stone, attaching it to the sides of the tomb with wax, which was then impressed with a royal signet ring.

This is the garden tomb where many believe Jesus was buried by both Joseph of Arimathea and Nicodemus.

New Testament Fulfillment

Jesus was to be buried with the two thieves, but a righteous Pharisee, Joseph of Arimathea, intervened (John 20:38). In doing so he made it possible for Jesus to be buried in a rich man's tomb, as Isaiah had prophesied.

"HE IS RISEN"
MARK 15:44-16:8

Old Testament Link
In Exodus 19 when God gave his Law to the Children of Israel on Mount Sinai, the scene was one of lightning and the trembling of the earth. The Law would also provide a sacrifice at the Temple where those who drew near might find atonement for sin and reconciliation with God.

Jesus was dead. This is what the disciples believed, never expecting to see Him again. On many occasions Jesus had predicted His resurrection on the third day, but the idea had not taken root in their minds (John 20:9).

From Friday evening, when Joseph of Arimathea and Nicodemus placed Him in the garden tomb, until early Sunday morning, His body lay in the small six feet by six feet stone chamber.

At dawn of the third day, Mary Magdalene, with some other women, came to the tomb to further embalm the body with spices. Seeing the large stone that covered the tomb's entrance, they were perplexed.

"There was a violent earthquake, for an angel of the Lord came down from heaven and, going to the tomb, rolled back the stone and sat on it. His appearance was like lightning, and his clothes were white as snow. The guards were so afraid of him that they shook and became like dead men" (Matthew 28:2-4).

The angel rolled away the stone not so Jesus could leave the tomb, for He had already risen. Rather it was so Mary could enter and discover the tomb was empty.

"Don't be alarmed," the angel said. "...He has risen!...See the place where they laid him. But go, tell his disciples and Peter, 'He is going ahead of you into Galilee..." (Mark 16:6-7).

Mary raced to the house where the disciples were hiding. Peter and John rushed to the tomb and saw something even more startling. They saw Jesus' graveclothes and the cloth that had covered His face.

The Angel made special mention of Peter to Mary Magdalene to show that in spite of Peter's denials, Jesus had not denied him.

New Testament Fulfillment

On the day that Jesus rose from the dead there was lightning and the trembling of the earth. Once again God had made it possible for men to draw near and find atonement for their sins. When Moses brought the Law down from Mt. Sinai, 3000 men perished (Exodus 32:28), but when Peter proclaimed the risen Messiah, 3000 dead men came to experience eternal life (Acts 2:41).

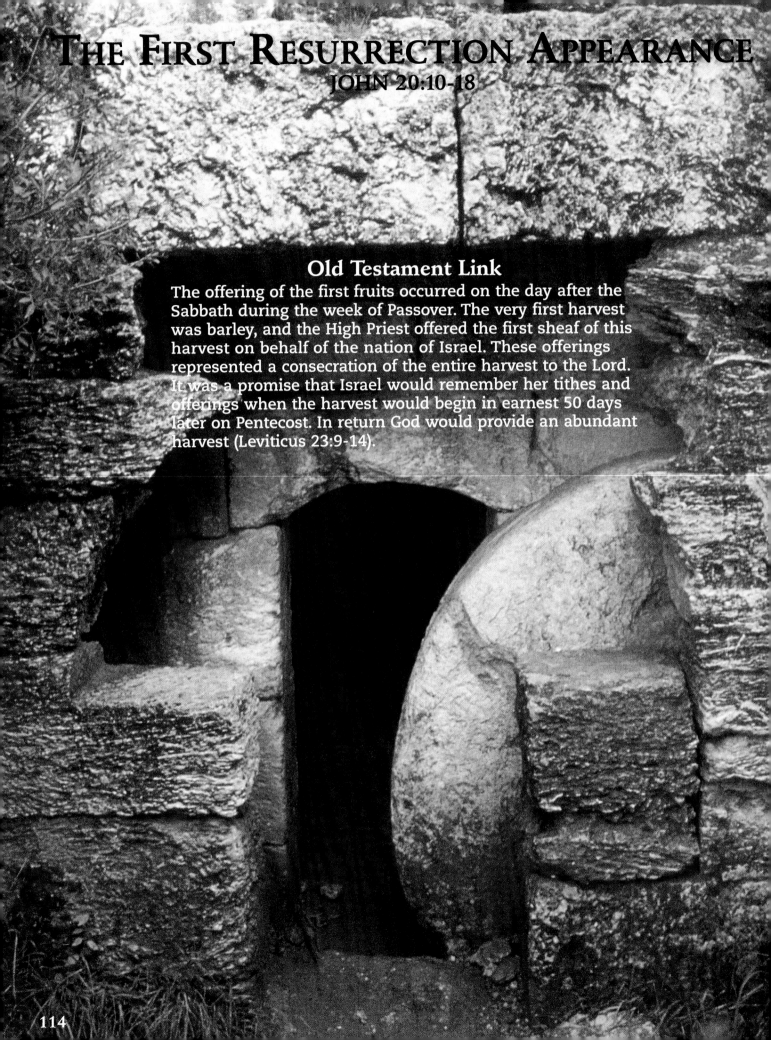

THE FIRST RESURRECTION APPEARANCE
JOHN 20:10-18

Old Testament Link
The offering of the first fruits occurred on the day after the Sabbath during the week of Passover. The very first harvest was barley, and the High Priest offered the first sheaf of this harvest on behalf of the nation of Israel. These offerings represented a consecration of the entire harvest to the Lord. It was a promise that Israel would remember her tithes and offerings when the harvest would begin in earnest 50 days later on Pentecost. In return God would provide an abundant harvest (Leviticus 23:9-14).

Even though Mary Magdalene had already been told by angelic heralds that Jesus had risen from the dead, she still doubted. Why else would she continue to weep outside the garden tomb?

Peering into the tomb, she supposed that the Messiah's body had been moved elsewhere. He had been condemned as a criminal, and many believed that a criminal could defile a tomb and ruin it. The fires in the Valley of Gehenna were reserved for the disposal of such criminal corpses. Mary wished to spare the body of the Lord from this shame; hence her frantic search for His corpse.

Whether she had been temporarily blinded by the brightness of the angels in the tomb or her eyes were clouded with tears, Mary did not recognize the Lord when He spoke to her: "Woman, why are you crying? Who is it you are looking for?" (John 20:15). Supposing that this figure was the gardener, she asked him where he had moved the body.

"Mary," Jesus said to her. Recognizing the manner in which He spoke her name she spun around and cried out: "Rabboni!" (Aramaic for teacher).

Mary clung to Him, desiring never to be separated from the Lord again. However, He could not have the fellowship with her as He had before. He had risen and His being had been transformed to a body that knew not the limits of space and time. Her fellowship with Him hereafter would not be governed by earthly confines but by the Spirit.

To make sure His followers believed He had truly been raised from the dead, Jesus appeared to Peter, James and the rest of the disciples, and to over 500 of the brothers.

New Testament Fulfillment

At the precise time that the High Priest was waving the sheaf of first fruits in the Holy Place in the Temple, the day after the Sabbath of Passover, Jesus rose from the dead. The resurrection of Jesus fulfilled what the offering of the first fruits symbolized; the beginning of the harvest. Since Christ rose from the dead and was consecrated to the Lord, He embodies a pledge that there will be a greater harvest (1 Corinthians 15:20-22).

Mary did not want to lose Jesus again. She had not understood the resurrection, but Jesus could not be detained at the tomb. He had important work to do.

THE APPEARANCE TO TWO TRAVELERS
LUKE 24:13-32

Old Testament Link

The promise of the Messiah originated immediately after the fall of Adam and Eve with God's words that One would "crush [Satan's] head" (Genesis 3:15). The Old Testament, beginning with Moses and continuing through the writings and the prophets, spoke of how Israel would recognize the One who would come to deliver Her and the world from the god of this world, Satan (Genesis 12:3, 49:10; Numbers 24:17; Deuteronomy 18:18).

While the disciples mourned and hid, unsure of their own fate and that of their Master's, two other followers of Jesus walked a dusty road seven miles from Jerusalem. As they made their way down the Emmaus Road, the events of the last few days — the amazing trial and subsequent crucifixion of Jesus — overwhelmed them. Trying to make sense of all that had transpired, they were deep in conversation when Jesus fell in step with them.

They failed to recognize Him, but His seeming ignorance of the recent events brought their full attention to Him. *How could He not know what had just happened in Jerusalem? How could He be unaware of how "The chief priests and...rulers handed Him over to be sentenced to death..."* (Luke 24:20).

Neither they nor the rabbis of Israel could understand the concept of a suffering Messiah, although the Talmud spoke of "two Messiahs."

One Messiah would come to suffer for the sins of Israel, Messiah Ben Joseph (fulfilled by Jesus' first coming). Another Messiah, Messiah Ben David (which will be fulfilled at His second coming), would come to reign. Messiah Ben Joseph, literally the son of Joseph, like his namesake would be misunderstood and cast out by his brethren. Messiah Ben David, like King David, would cloak himself in royal garb, judging the Israelites as King, vanquishing their

New Testament Fulfillment

Jesus walked with two travelers on the road to Emmaus, which most believe is located about seven miles northwest of Jerusalem. Jesus shared with them many of the Old Testament prophecies. Several writers of the New Testament noted that many of these prophecies were fulfilled (Matthew 1:23, 2:6, 4:14-16, 21:4-5; John 19:33-37).

enemies and ushering in the glorious Messianic Kingdom.

Jesus explained to his fellow travelers, "...beginning with Moses and all the Prophets..." (Luke 24:27), how the Messiah needed to first atone for the sins of Israel and mankind and then enter into glory.

The travelers invited Him to stay the evening. As He broke bread with them, perhaps the manner in which He prayed and gave thanks caused them to finally recognize the identity of their visitor. They had seen the resurrected Jesus, the victorious Messiah. In a short moment, all became clear to them. Then, "He disappeared from their sight" (Luke 24:31).

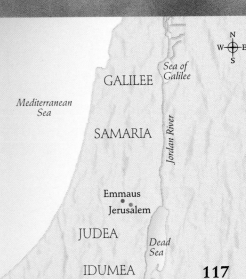

Two of Jesus' followers, walking from Jerusalem on the road to Emmaus, encountered a stranger. After revealing Himself to them, Jesus disappeared.

THE ASCENSION
ACTS 1:9-12

Old Testament Link
"Blessed is he who comes in the name of the Lord" (Psalm 118:26). While many Jewish people accepted Jesus as the promised Messiah, the majority did not. Jesus, the Hope of Israel, will remain in heaven until the nation and its leadership is prepared to mourn for Him (Zechariah 12:10).

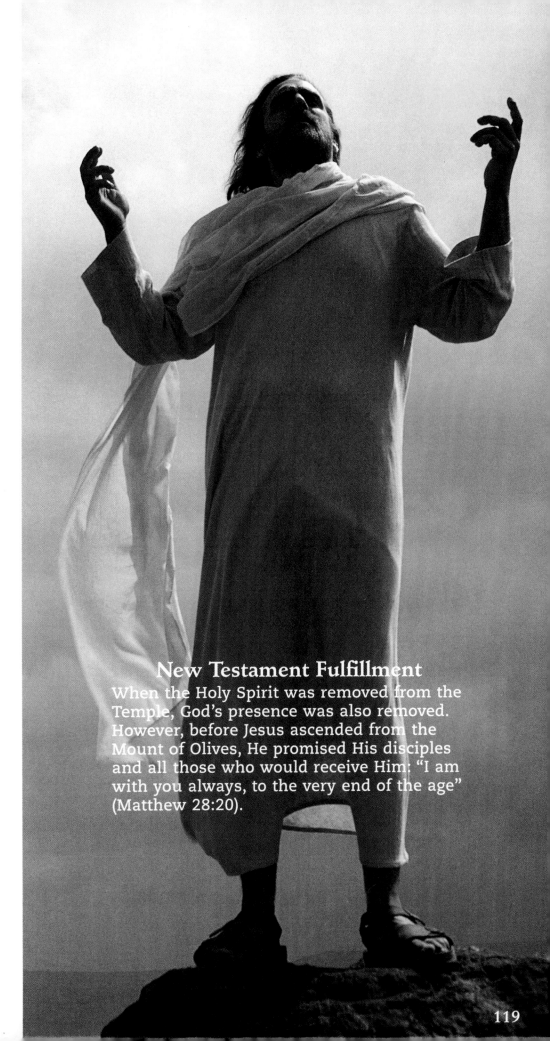

For 40 days after His resurrection, Jesus appeared and met with His disciples often. Just as He opened the minds of the Emmaus Road travelers, He explained to the disciples the meaning and fulfillment of Scripture. In His final commission, He gave them the authority to assure the forgiveness of sin through the finished atonement He had provided.

Leaving Jerusalem, heading toward Bethany, Jesus stopped on the slope of the Mount of Olives and faced the Eastern Gate of the Temple. Hundreds of years earlier, Ezekiel had witnessed the Spirit of the Lord departing the Temple from this gate (Eziekel 9:3; 10:18-19). Only days before His crucifixion, Jesus, too, had left the Temple from this gate. The ancient rabbinic sages had always believed that the Messiah would return through this gate (Golden Gate), when He finally comes to defend Israel from those who seek to destroy it.

Unsure and still thinking of an earthly kingdom, the disciples asked Him: "Lord, are you at this time going to restore the kingdom to Israel?" (Acts 1:6). Jesus once again drew their attention to the part they would play as His representatives on earth, not only as eyewitnesses to His death and resurrection, but as men empowered to offer the gift of salvation to both Jew and Gentile.

"After He said this, He was taken up before their very eyes, in a cloud that hid Him from their sight. They were looking intently up into the sky as He was ascending, when suddenly two men dressed in white stood beside them. 'Men of Galilee,' they said, 'why do you stand here looking into the sky? This same Jesus, who has been taken from you into heaven, will come back in the same way you have seen him go into heaven'" (Acts 1:9-11).

The Mount of Olives, shown as it is today, was the site of the Ascension.

New Testament Fulfillment

When the Holy Spirit was removed from the Temple, God's presence was also removed. However, before Jesus ascended from the Mount of Olives, He promised His disciples and all those who would receive Him: "I am with you always, to the very end of the age" (Matthew 28:20).

119

THOSE WHO WALKED WITH JESUS

THE VIRGIN MARY, THE MOTHER OF JESUS

Mary's mission in life was to be the chosen Jewish virgin who would bear the promised Messiah and raise Him. From the days of His birth the words of John could be applied to her: "He must become greater; I must become less" (John 3:30). Simeon rightly prophesied her fate when he said that a sword would pierce her soul, referring to the agony she would endure at His death. The mother-son relationship ended as Jesus was giving His life for sin on the cross. In John 19:25-27, Jesus gave John to her as a son. Soon He would reveal Himself to her and the world as the Lord and Savior.

In all likelihood she died of old age in the home of the apostle John, her appointed son.

JOSEPH, THE HUSBAND OF MARY

Before the birth of Jesus, Joseph lived in Nazareth as a poor craftsman working primarily in stone. As a direct descendant of King David and Solomon, he was a pious and religious man (Matthew 1:18-25). Three times God directly communicated with him: (1) to assure him of his betrothed's purity and to take her as his wife; (2) after the visit of the Magi, when he was told to take the mother and child to Egypt; (3) when he was told to return to Israel. His poverty is evident at the dedication of Jesus when his offering in the Temple consisted of only two turtle doves.

The last mention of Joseph is when Jesus was 12 years old in the Temple. Joseph probably died before Jesus began His earthly ministry, for he is not present at the wedding at Cana or anytime later.

JOHN THE BAPTIST

John was of priestly descent; his mother was one of the "daughters of Aaron" and his father was a priest (Luke 1:5). His parents were well advanced in years and died while he was young. Some believe that he may have been raised by the community of Qumran. According to Josephus, Herod Antipas feared that John would fan the flames of revolt against Rome. To prevent a riot, Herod seized John and imprisoned him. The account of John testifies that the Baptist was jailed for rebuking Herod for marrying his brother's wife, Herodias.

John was beheaded at the request of Herod's step-daughter, Salome (Matthew 14:6-13).

ANDREW

In Greek, Andreas means "manly" or "mighty one." Andrew was one of the 12 disciples of Jesus Christ and the brother of Simon, called Peter. A Galilean fisherman of Bethsaida, Andrew was originally a disciple of John the Baptist. In the Gospel of John, he was the first called to be a disciple of Jesus. He was likely present at the wedding of Cana (John 2:2), but then appears to have returned to fishing. He received a second call to follow Jesus after the imprisonment of John the Baptist (Matthew 4:12-20).

According to tradition, Andrew was crucified at Patmos, in Achaia, on an X-shaped cross, the form of which became known as the St. Andrew's Cross. He is the patron saint of Scotland and Russia.

PETER

In all the listings of he 12 disciples, Peter is always listed first, because of his appointed role as leader. He was also part of Jesus' inner circle of disciples along with ames and John. Apart from the name of Jesus, Peter's name is mentioned most often in the New Testament. He speaks the most, was reproved the most and once was so presumptuous he rebuked the Lord. He boldly confessed his faith, yet in similar fashion denied the Lord. Peter was the most highly praised by the Lord and yet the only one Jesus rebuked as if he were Satan (Matthew 16:23).

He had many qualities that were necessary for leadership. Peter traveled extensively in his missionary activity, accompanied by his wife.

His death was ordered by Emperor Nero in 64 A.D. According to tradition, Peter requested to be crucified upside down, believing himself unworthy to die the same way as his Lord.

JAMES

James is the English equivalent of the Greek *Iakobos*, which comes from the Hebrew *Yacov*, or Jacob. Both James and John, his brother, were likely known for their tempers, hence their nicknames, "Sons of Thunder." James was one of Jesus' inner circle of disciples and accompanied Jesus, Peter and John to the Mount of Transfiguration.

According to a 17th-century tradition, James is said to have visited Spain before his martyrdom. When Herod Agrippa I wanted to attack the infant Christian Church, James was executed. James became the first apostle to be martyred (Acts 12:1:3).

JOHN

Next to Peter, John was the most prominent of the disciples. His long life demonstrates his transformation by the Holy Spirit from being a "Son of Thunder" to the apostle of love. One account states that John did not leave the city of Jerusalem until Mary, the mother of Jesus, died, because the Lord entrusted her to John's care (John 19:27). Others suggested that he took her with him to Ephesus where he ministered. Many believe Mary's tomb is also in Ephesus. The belief that John died of old age has been attributed to the account in John's Gospel (John 21:22).

Most believe John was banished to the small, barren isle of Patmos in the west coast of Asia Minor. Here he wrote the message of the Book of Revelations, which ties Old Testament End Time prophecy with the New Covenant. According to that tradition, he died there in 98 A.D.

NICODEMUS

A Pharisee and a member of the Sanhedrin, Nicodemus is only mentioned three times in the Gospel of John. The first concerns the discussion of the new birth (John 3:1-10). His night meeting with Jesus demonstrated his fear of being seen by his peers with Him. His own word declared his belief that Jesus was a teacher sent by God. He challenged the Sanhedrin when they wanted to condemn Jesus without a formal hearing (John 7:50). As a result, the leaders accused him of being a follower of Jesus. Finally, Nicodemus boldly joined Joseph of Arimathea, attending to the burial of Jesus (John 19:38).

Tradition accounts his baptism and the hardships that he later encountered for his faith, including his banishment from Jerusalem. He eventually died outside of the city that had meant so much to him.

MARTHA

Her name in Aramaic is *Marta,* meaning lady or mistress of the house. Martha was the sister of Lazarus and Mary and lived in Bethany (Luke 10:38-42). Martha was the oldest sibling and as such lived up to her name. It was Martha who bore the responsibility for meeting and entertaining Jesus when He came to visit. Like an older sister who wearied of bearing all the work, she asked Jesus to tell Mary to help her. Jesus gently chided her about her worries. Scripture tells us that Jesus loved Martha, Mary and Lazarus (John 11:5). It was Martha who approached Jesus after the death of Lazarus and had faith to believe He could raise her brother from the dead.

Nothing is known concerning when and how she died.

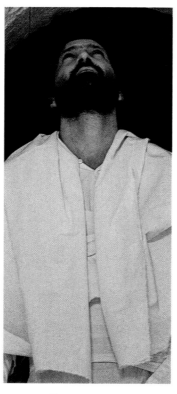

LAZARUS

The brother of Mary and Martha was an intimate friend of Jesus. He is mentioned only in John 11 and 12, which contain the description of Jesus' raising him from the dead. The family lived in Bethany located on the southeast side of the Mount of Olives. Jesus purposely delayed going to Lazarus after being told about his sickness for two days. He told His disciples: "This sickness will not end in death. No, it is for God's glory so that God's Son may be glorified through it" (John 11:4). Raising Lazarus from the dead further established His credentials as the promised Messiah.

According to an Eastern tradition, in an attempt to put them to death, Lazarus and his sisters were put in a leaking boat on the Mediterranean, but reached the island of Cyprus. There he became bishop of Kitium.

MARY, THE SISTER OF MARTHA AND LAZARUS

The most notable characteristic of Mary is her tender worship and submission to Jesus. While Martha was busy making preparations for serving Jesus, Mary sat at the feet of Jesus listening to everything He said. Martha asked Jesus to tell Mary to help. Jesus responded that Mary chose to do what was best (Luke 10:38-42). Mary anointed Jesus with expensive perfume. She was deeply devoted to the Lord. Jesus said prophetically of her: "I tell you the truth, wherever the gospel is preached throughout the world, what she has done will also be told, in memory of her" (Mark 14:9).

Legend records that Mary joined her sister Martha and brother Lazarus traveling to the island of Cyprus where she died.

THOMAS

In Aramaic the name *Teoma* means twin, and in the Gospel of John he is referred to as Thomas called *Didymus,* which is the Greek word for twin. The name Thomas was probably a nickname. Known for his doubting nature, he should also be recognized for his courage. In John 11:16 he said: "Let us also go, that we may die with Him." Thomas is also known for his great confession in John 20:28 where he confessed Christ's divinity by saying, "My Lord, my God."

Most traditions claim he traveled to Persia and Southern India where he founded the Mar Thoma Church, and was martyred there.

JUDAS ISCARIOT

The name *Iscariot* could have come from a few different sources. The most obvious is from the Hebrew, literally "man from Kerioth." A second could come from the Aramaic root *"sqr"* which means "liar," and with the prefix *"ish"* could be translated "man of the lie." The Scriptures tell us that Judas betrayed Jesus under the direction of Satan (Luke 22:3; John 13:2). A different theory suggests that Judas truly did believe Christ was the promised Messiah, but sought to force His hand by turning Him over to the authorities. This would force Him to react and establish His Kingdom. The Books of Matthew, Mark and Luke represent Jesus as being fully aware of this conscious premeditated treachery, which He foretold.

When Judas saw the consequences of his act, he was filled with despair and hung himself. The New Testament contains two different accounts of his death (Matthew 27:3-5; Acts 1:16-20).

PONTIUS PILATE

He was the Roman military governor, or procurator, of the province of Judea from 26 to 36 A.D. The Jewish historian Flavius Josephus portrayed him as a harsh administrator who failed to understand the religious convictions and national pride of the Jews.

Pilate was recalled to Rome in 36 A.D. to stand trial for an incident that occurred in Samaria. Various traditions relate the execution of Pilate by Nero, his banishment to Vienna or him taking his own life.

According to the theologian and church historian Eusebius of Caesarea, Pilate committed suicide during the reign of Gaius (37-41 A.D.). In all likelihood this occurred after his trial and condemnation for the slaughter of Samaritan fanatics.

HEROD ANTIPAS

Herod Antipas was one of the sons of Herod the Great, born in 20 B.C. Antipas was tetrarch over Galilee and Perea, the chief areas of ministry for John the Baptist and Jesus. Antipas had fallen in love with Herodias, the wife of his half-brother Philip. She desired to be married to Herod because of his political power and influence, and agreed to marry him if he would divorce his present wife. John the Baptist spoke out against the union and was imprisoned by Antipas. It was at Herodias' urging that her daughter asked for the head of John the Baptist on a platter (Matthew 14:3-12). Jesus is later brought for trial before Antipas (Luke 23:6-12).

In 36 A.D., Aretas, the father of Antipas' first wife, attacked and defeated Antipas. The attack was revenge for the treatment of his daughter who was rejected so that Antipas could marry Herodias. Antipas never regained his kingdom and died in exile with his wife in Southern France.

JOSEPH OF ARIMATHEA

According to all four Gospels of the New Testament, Joseph was a wealthy Jewish man who was a member of the Sanhedrin, the ancient Jewish court in Jerusalem. He boldly took a stand demonstrating his sympathy for Jesus by requesting from Pontius Pilate if he could take Jesus' body and place it in his own tomb. He is described as one who became a disciple of Jesus (Matthew 27:57). Joseph was joined by Nicodemus in the burial of Jesus (John 19:38-39).

Legends from a later period report that Joseph was sent by the apostle Philip from Gaul to England where he built the first church in Glastonbury. In 1135, the English historian William of Malmesbury, in an account of the ancient church of Glastonbury in Somerset, recorded the story of Joseph of Arimathea's voyage to England, bringing the holy chalice, or grail, used at the Last Supper.

NATHANIEL

Nathaniel (known also as Bartholomew) was a native of Cana of Galilee, and was one of the 12 disciples of Jesus. In John 21:2 he is mentioned as being one of the eyewitnesses of Jesus' resurrection. In John's account we are told Jesus said of Nathaniel that he was an Israelite in whom there was no guile. He was part of the minority who not only was a Jew outwardly, but inwardly as well (Romans 2:29, 9:6-8, Galations 6:16). When Jesus complemented his honesty, Nathaniel did not become proud, but wondered how He knew him. It was then that Jesus told that He saw him under the fig tree (John 1:48).

He traveled as far as India and was flayed alive at Albanoplolis in Armenia.

THADDAEUS

The name Thaddaeus is the Greek form of the Hebrew *Lebbaeus,* whose root is "heart." It was a nickname that connotated endearment. His given name was in all likelihood Judas. In Scripture he is sometimes referred to as "Judas the son of James" (Luke 6:16, John 14:22, Acts 1:13). Tradition teaches that Thaddaeus traveled after the ascension of Jesus to minister among the people of Edessa in Mesopotamia and to their king, Abgar, who had previously written to Jesus asking that He come to Mesopotamia. Thaddaeus is said to have performed miracles and taught the Way of Life to both Jews and Gentiles, baptizing many. Furthermore, he planted a number of churches, appointing bishops and deacons to lead them. Eusebius, the historian, wrote that Thaddaeus ministered in the Mesopotamian city of Amis and died in Berytus of Phonecia, which is the modern city of Beirut.

JAMES, THE SON OF ALPHAEUS

In Mark 15:40 he is referred to as James the Less, which probably refers to his being younger than the other apostle James, the Son of Zebedee. Matthew's father is also recorded as being Alphaeus (Mark 2:14). This would lead to the accepted idea that James was the brother of Matthew.

The early Church Fathers claimed that James preached in Persia, and was martyred by crucifixion there.

MATTHEW

Matthew, also known as Levi, was a tax collector, despised because he collected money for Rome and made a profit from his own kinsmen. A reference in the Talmud says: "It is righteous to lie and deceive a tax collector." Tax collectors were fully protected and supported by the Roman army. When Matthew left his business of collecting taxes there was no turning back. Unlike the fishermen who followed Jesus, Matthew could not return to his old profession.

It is remarkable that this disciple, who was so despised as an outcast to the Jewish community, would write the gospel account that cites the most Old Testament Scriptures.

Later, legendary accounts tell of Matthew's travel to Ethiopia where he became associated with Candace, identified with the eunuch of Acts 8:27, and was eventually martyred.

PHILIP

Philip was the first disciple called by Jesus (John 1:43). Philip was a native of Bethsaida, a small town on the north shore of the Sea of Galilee. This was also the hometown of Andrew and Peter. Philip found Nathaniel and told him that he had discovered the Messiah, Jesus of Nazareth (John 1:45). Philip is a Greek name meaning "lover of horses." When the Greeks wanted to see the Jews, they approached Philip, probably because of his Hellenistic roots. Philip left John the Baptist to follow Jesus. He is mentioned in John 6:5-7, 12:21-22, 14:8-14.

Polycrates, a 2nd century bishop, said Philip ministered in the Roman province of Asia and was martyred by being crucified upside down and buried at Hierapolis.

SIMON THE ZEALOT

The term *zealot* denotes that Simon was a member of the political party called the Zealots, which sought to rid Israel of the yoke of Rome. These Zealots were the ideological offspring of the Maccabees, who rebelled against Syrian oppression and rededicated the Temple in 168 B.C. Zealots, like the Maccabees, were guerrilla fighters who would launch attacks against the Roman occupiers and retreat to the hills to hide. Simon, however, remained faithful to the Lord and was listed as one of the 12 apostles.

According to tradition, Simon preached in Persia where he was martyred for his faith.

MARY MAGDALENE

The name Magdalene was derived from Magdala, a town on the western shore of the Sea of Galilee. Mary is mentioned in Luke 8:2. After Jesus delivered her from demons, she became a devoted follower. A wealthy woman, Mary supported the ministry of Jesus from her own resources (Luke 8:1-3). When the disciples fled from Jesus, Mary remained with Him, following Him to the cross, and then watching to see where He would be buried (Mark 15:40-47). Mary was one of the first to bring spices for the burial of Jesus (Matthew 28:1). It was Mary who ran to tell Peter that the tomb was empty and then returned. After seeing the Lord, she was told to tell the disciples He had risen (John 20:17).

According to church tradition she traveled with John to Ephesus, where she died and her body taken to Constantinople.

SAMARITAN WOMAN

The remarkable encounter between Jesus and this woman is related in John 4. Samaritans were despised by the Jewish people. The reason for this dates from the time of the split between Judah and Israel. Ezra and Nehemiah recount the obstacles that the Samaritans placed in the way of a Jewish revival. They were hated because they had intermarried and were of mixed blood. That Jesus would speak to a Samaritan went against a long standing tradition. This woman, who was an outcast even to her own people, was the object of the love and compassion of Jesus. She was the first Samaritan to hear the gospel from the mouth of the Messiah, thus foreshadowing the Great Commission of Acts 1:8.

THE LAND WHERE JESUS WALKED

N
W · E
S

To Rome

Mt. Hermon

Caesarea Philippi

GALILEE

Capernaum

Bethsaida

Cana

Gennesaret

Sea
of Galilee

Nazareth

Mt. Tabor

Mediterranean
Sea

SAMARIA

Samaria

Jordan River

Decapolis
(Ten Towns)

Mt. of Olives

Emmaus

Jericho

Jerusalem

Bethany

Bethlehem

JUDEA

Dead
Sea

IDUMEA

To Egypt

JERUSALEM AND THE TEMPLE IN THE TIME OF JESUS

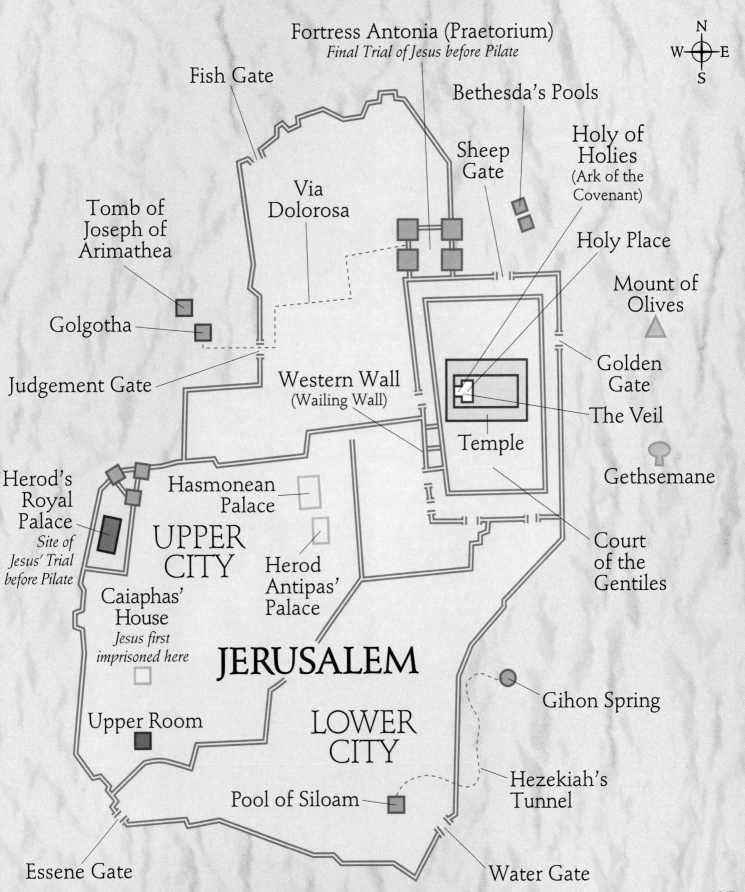

Fortress Antonia (Praetorium)
Final Trial of Jesus before Pilate

Fish Gate

Bethesda's Pools

Sheep Gate

Holy of Holies
(Ark of the Covenant)

Via Dolorosa

Holy Place

Tomb of Joseph of Arimathea

Mount of Olives

Golgotha

Golden Gate

Judgement Gate

Western Wall (Wailing Wall)

The Veil

Temple

Herod's Royal Palace
Site of Jesus' Trial before Pilate

Hasmonean Palace

Court of the Gentiles

Gethsemane

UPPER CITY

Caiaphas' House
Jesus first imprisoned here

Herod Antipas' Palace

JERUSALEM

Gihon Spring

Upper Room

LOWER CITY

Hezekiah's Tunnel

Essene Gate

Pool of Siloam

Water Gate

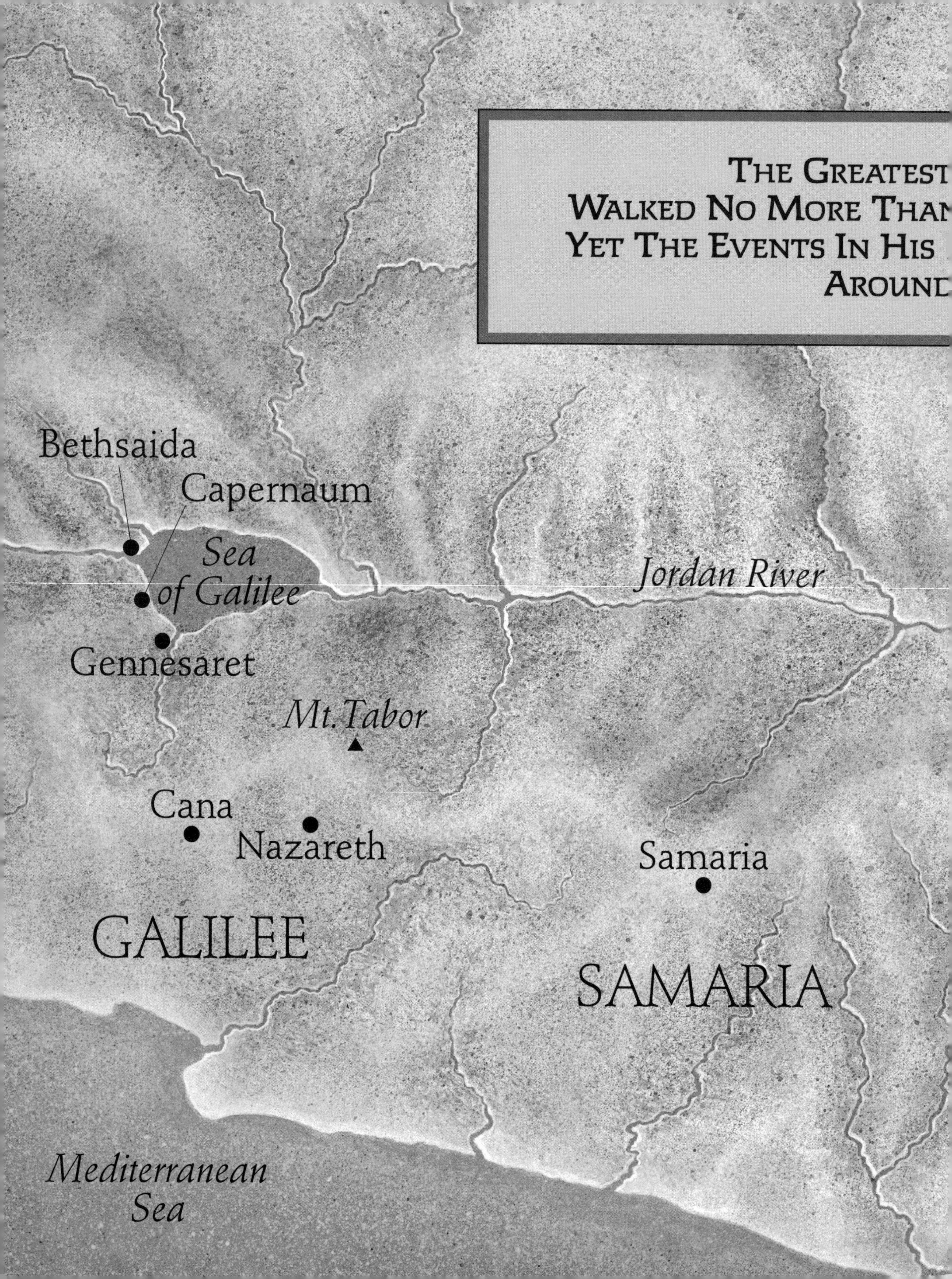

THE GREATEST
WALKED NO MORE THA
YET THE EVENTS IN HIS
AROUN
Bethsaida
Capernaum
Sea of Galilee
Jordan River
Gennesaret
Mt.Tabor
Cana
Nazareth
Samaria
GALILEE
SAMARIA
Mediterranean Sea